IT IS TIME

By
VANCE HAVNER
Author of "Rest a While," "Consider Him," "Road to Revival," "The Secret of Christian Joy," "By the Still Waters"

New York
FLEMING H. REVELL COMPANY
London and Edinburgh

Printed in the United States of America

New York: 158 Fifth Avenue
London: 99 Anerley Road

FOREWORD

IN these sermons on the times, the reader will discover that I am not entering into the intricacies of interpreting prophecy. Rather, these awful days through which we are passing are viewed in the light of those Scriptures which reveal the broad, general trend of God's purposes as revealed in His Word. The main burden of the book is God's call to revival among His people.

Acknowledgment is made to *Revelation Magazine* of Philadelphia for permission to reprint "It Is Time" and "Later Than You Think"; to the *Moody Monthly* of Chicago for the use of "Watchman, What of the Night?" and "Time to Wake Up"; to *King's Business* of Los Angeles for "Time to Be Sober"; and to *Our Hope* of New York for "Time for Judgment." There has been, however, considerable revision of these articles, made necessary by the subject matter.

In this tragic day, when many magicians and soothsayers are trying to read the handwriting on the wall, it is hoped that these messages may incline some to listen to the Daniel of God's Word and to act accordingly.

V. H.

Greensboro, N. C.

CONTENTS

I

WHAT TIME IS IT?

*"Watchman, what of the night? Watchman, what of the night?
The watchman said, The morning cometh, and also the night: if ye
will enquire, enquire ye: return, come."*—ISAIAH 21: 11, 12.

I AM aware of the fact that this text has come in for
plenty of use and misuse in these troublous times. It
has been made a convenient subject for wild and weird
prophets who know more about the future than the Bible has
ever revealed. It has been a favorite headline for sensational
scribblers who take advantage of these terrible days to peddle
crackpot theories never heard before on land or sea. Even
some politicians have borrowed the verse from a Bible they
never read to give a religious color to an otherwise ungodly
speech.

But no matter how well-worn my text may be, it never
was more timely. We certainly are in the middle of a pitch-
black moral and spiritual night. We need a watchman.
And we need to know what of the night.

The text suggests a watchman. God's prophets are His
watchmen. He told Ezekiel: "Son of man, I have made
thee a watchman unto the house of Israel" (3: 17). From
Enoch to John on Patmos He appointed men to foretell
and forthtell His purpose through the ages. He has never
abolished the work of the prophet-watchman, for "God hath
set some in the church, first apostles, secondarily prophets"
(1 Cor. 12: 28). They are His watchdogs, for He calls
false watchmen "dumb dogs that cannot bark" (Isa.
56: 10–12). A watchdog that will not bark is not worth
having, and a preacher who will not warn men of sin is a
traitor within the camp. "He that is an hireling, and not
the shepherd, whose own the sheep are not, seeth the wolf

[7]

coming, and leaveth the sheep, and fleeth: and the wolf catcheth them, and scattereth the sheep. The hireling fleeth, because he is an hireling, and careth not for the sheep " (John 10: 12, 13).

Every pastor is God's watchman, for he watches for men's souls as they that must give account (Heb. 13: 17). And if a man claims to be a watchman, it is expected of him that he should know something about the night: how we got into it, where we are, and where we go from here. There are too many Hananiahs who make the people to believe a lie and not enough Micaiahs who say: " What the Lord saith unto me, that will I speak." When God has told us the meaning of our times, then to stand with an open Bible in one hand and a newspaper in the other and not know the time of day is criminal. Too many prophets are not up on the watchtower; they are down in the basement exactly like the false watchmen Isaiah described: " Come ye, say they, I will fetch wine, and we will fill ourselves with strong drink; and tomorrow shall be as this day, and much more abundant " (Isa. 56: 12). " Nothing to be excited about. Everything will come out all right. All this talk about the Lord's return is just a nervous reaction from these tense times." Our Lord described the same case in the servant who said, " My Lord delayeth his coming," and began to beat the servants and to eat and drink and be drunken. And Jesus expressly declared that such a man would be cut off and appointed his portion with unbelievers (Lk. 12: 45, 46). There are men who claim to be God's watchmen who dismiss the whole subject of Bible prophecy as though it were a jigsaw puzzle for nitwits to worry about.

I grant you that there are false watchmen of another sort who have gone to seed on prophecy, who read into the Bible what is not there and read out of it what is there, who see bugaboos and hobgoblins and cry " Wolf " when there is no wolf. Some of these alarmists are the sort who picked out

Mussolini for the Antichrist, and are now spending their time trying to rescue their reputations. But for every false watchman of this kind who cries "Wolf" when there is no wolf, there are a hundred who preach peace when there is no peace. And God is saying of these professional "take-it-easy" crooners trying to lull a sick world to sleep with social gospel bedtime stories, "Hearken not unto the words of the prophets that prophesy unto you: they make you vain: they speak a vision of their own heart, and not out of the mouth of the Lord" (Jer. 23: 16). The faithful watchman is called a pessimist, a pulpit hoot owl, but Micah was willing to be a hoot-owl preacher, "I will make . . . mourning as the owls" (1: 8). Better be God's hoot owl than the devil's mockingbird!

The text sets before us not only a *watchman* but also the *night*. It is evident to all who have eyes to see that we are in the midst of moral and spiritual, social and political, national and international darkness. It is enough simply to stand with our Bibles opened at the third chapter of Second Timothy and look out on the maddening whirl of these awful days. I see nations tottering in a world gone crazy; and I read, "In the last days perilous times shall come." I see men living for self and none beside, just as if Jesus had never lived, just as if He had never died; and I read, "Men shall be lovers of their own selves." I see men living for what they can grab, not what they can give; and I read that men shall be "covetous"; I hear men boast of human greatness while civilization tumbles on our heads; and I read that men shall be "proud, boasters, heady, high-minded." I behold nations at war against God; I read of parties in our own land where men come representing different gods and some representing Almighty God; and I read that men shall be "blasphemers." I see a young generation without authority inside or out, our home life a thing of the past; and I read that men shall be "disobedient to parents."

I behold a land that has struck sex o'clock, that is up to its ears in slop and sophistication, petting dogs instead of children, and rotten with social diseases; and I read that men shall be " unholy, without natural affection . . . incontinent." I see our jails filled with young hoodlums, our crime rate the disgrace of civilization, with cutthroats living in mansions and gangsters in high places; and I read that " evil men . . . shall wax worse and worse," that men shall be " fierce, despisers of those that are good." I notice that a man's word means nothing today, that business contracts, marriage vows, and national treaties are only scraps of paper; and I read that men shall be " trucebreakers." I see pleasure resorts jammed, theaters and stadiums packed, night clubs crowded, while a corporal's guard holds forth at the house of the Lord; and I read that men shall be " lovers of pleasures more than lovers of God."

I visit the churches and find that saints who were born in revival fires are living in the smoke; that meeting-houses have become mausoleums, and that the glory has departed from the sanctuary; and I read that men shall have a form of godliness but deny the power thereof. Sardis has a name to be alive but is dead; the icicles of indifference hang over churches that ought to be melted in the fires of God. Truly, the night is upon us. God is writing on the wall; the astrologers and soothsayers cannot read it and men will not believe Daniel; even some preachers ignore him although our Lord called special attention to him and advised us to read up on what Daniel had to say. " Ye hypocrites, ye can discern the face of the sky; but can ye not discern the signs of the times? " (Matt. 16: 3).

The text presents next a momentous question: " Watchman, WHAT OF THE NIGHT? " and a double answer, " THE MORNING COMETH, AND ALSO THE

NIGHT." Is the world growing better or worse? It is growing both better and worse. The wheat and the tares both are growing until harvest. Real Christians are turning back to their Bibles, drawing nearer to God, separating from evil, witnessing to Christ. There is the sound of a going in the mulberry trees. Bible schools, Bible conferences, radio preachers, youth movements, laymen's movements, all are a sign that the Spirit of God is stirring among the saints. God is in the sifting business these days. He is drawing unto Himself out of all the churches those Christians who mean business with Him and separating them from the great mass of Sunday-morning churchgoers who have never caught on to what it is all about. As the night grows darker, these Christians grow brighter, and for them "the morning cometh" because Christ will return for His own.

But the world itself is growing worse. Evil men are waxing worse and worse. The mystery of lawlessness heads up to its awful climax, and the apostate church grows larger and larger. Don't be deceived because once in a while a Catholic priest, a Jewish rabbi, and a Protestant preacher unite in a union service. That is not a sign that the world is growing better. It is a sign that it is growing worse. When church groups begin uniting, that is usually a sign of weakness, not strength. They are getting so weak individually that they have to bunch up in self-defense. When you are sick and several doctors hold a consultation, it is not always a sign that you are up against a predicament: sometimes it is a sign that the doctors are! Sometimes they are puzzled and have to get their heads together on the basis that in unity there is strength. And don't get the idea that the millennium is just around the corner because some infidel writes a nice piece about Jesus. The tragedy of today is that too many people are saying nice things about Jesus and doing nothing for Him. They are complimenting Him, but not confessing Him.

[11]

The world is growing worse, and for the world " the night cometh," the night of judgment and tribulation. We read that at the last supper Judas went out, " and it was night " (John 13: 30). The world has gone out with its back turned on Jesus, and away from Jesus it is always night. The night of this world's distress will be followed by the night of eternal separation from God. The world has plenty of trouble today but nothing to compare with what faces it. " If thou hast run with the footmen, and they have wearied thee, then how canst thou contend with horses? and if in the land of peace, wherein thou trustedst, they wearied thee, then how wilt thou do in the swelling of Jordan? " (Jer. 12: 5). " For the time is come that judgment must begin at the house of God: and if it first begin at us, what shall the end be of them that obey not the gospel of God? And if the righteous scarcely be saved, where shall the ungodly and the sinner appear? " (1 Pet. 4: 17, 18). " The morning cometh " for the believer, " and also the night " for the unbeliever, with the sun turning black, the moon changing to blood, the stars falling like untimely figs, judgment breaking, the books opening—the eternal night of the second death, with fire unquenchable and the undying worm of everlasting misery in the agony of endless despair. For men who choose darkness rather than light in this present world must endure darkness forever.

God has told us what to expect. There is absolutely no reason for wringing our hands and wondering what we are coming to. We have the Word of God, which tells us where we came from, where we are, and where we are going. The churches are at sea today because they have lost their perspective. They refuse to believe that God is not out to convert the world, but to take out a people for His Name. If we don't know where we are headed, we don't know what to do where we are. I know that some serious-minded Christians have been scared away from the subject of prophecy by the antics of some prophecy preachers. But the same thing might be said of sanctification or any other Bible doctrine. And the issue is bigger and broader than pre- and post-millennialism. The issue is between two different viewpoints of the plan and purpose of God through the ages. It boils down to this: Will the preaching of the Gospel and the work of the churches gradually win this world to Christ, until evil is mastered by righteousness and the devil is put out of business? Or will the world steadily grow worse while God calls out a people to Himself, until Christ returns personally and suddenly to rule and reign? Here are two entirely different viewpoints, and they cannot possibly be brought together, for they are antithetical, not complementary. No man can possibly be working for both at the same time, nor can two looking in absolutely opposite directions work together for the Lord. It would require a spiritual cross-eyedness that reminds me of the boy who could hunt rabbits and squirrels at the same time, one eye looking up in the trees for squirrels, the other watching the ground for rabbits.

The plain fact is that evil must run its awful course, and then Christ is coming: and the main question is, How will He find me when He comes? Some He will find SCOFF-ING, saying, "Where is the promise of his coming?" (2 Pet. 3: 4). One hears even from some pulpit the very arguments Peter said the scoffers would use: "Since the fathers fell asleep, all things continue as they were from the beginning of the creation." In other words, "people have been excited before and thought Jesus was coming. History runs along about the same and today is nothing unusual." It is true that people have been mistaken before about the Lord's return. But while this sign and that have appeared through the years, there has never been the combination of signs that has converged upon us today. And while just at this moment everything is in such a confusion that it is impossible to figure out details because nations go out of business or change sides overnight, the main mark of the hour is that the whole world has reached such a hopeless situation that absolutely nothing but Divine intervention can begin to untangle the insane scramble. We have reached the point where only Almighty God can assemble the jig-saw puzzle of this crazy generation. Any man who can stand in such a day and speak lightly of the signs of the times is himself a sign of the end, for " there shall come in the last days SCOFFERS, walking after their own lusts."

While some will be SCOFFING when our Lord returns, others will be taken up with SURFEITING. "And take heed to yourselves, lest at any time your hearts be overcharged with surfeiting, and drunkenness, and cares of this life, and so that day come upon you unawares" (Lk. 21: 34). Here are those who say, "My lord delayeth his coming" and begin to beat the servants, to eat and drink and be drunken (Lk. 12: 45). Was there ever a word that described better this generation? Would you not think that in such an hour, with the foundations crumbling, with humanity wallowing in blood and tears, churches would be crowded and men setting their houses in order and getting right with God? Far from it; revelry and not repentance is the spirit of the age. America is at the night club, not at the prayer meeting. Even the saints have caught the fever and Christianity has been made a frolic instead of a fight, a picnic instead of a pilgrimage. The only fire left in many a church is down in the kitchen, where a defeated handful pour hot chocolate and read the minutes of the last meeting in a cheap imitation of the clubs of this world. " But this I say, brethren, the time is short: it remaineth, that both they that have wives be as though they had none; and they that weep, as though they wept not; and they that rejoiced as though they rejoiced not; and they that buy, as though they possessed not; and they that use this world, as not abusing it: for the fashion of this world passeth away (1 Cor. 7: 29–31). Surely in the face of such a verse, tone it down as you will, we need to watch and be sober, lest that day catch us eating and drinking as in the days of Noah.

Still others will be SLEEPING. "And that, knowing the time, that now it is high time to awake out of sleep: for now is our salvation nearer than when we believed" (Rom. 13: 11). I have observed in the past few years that a strange stupor has fallen over the church of God. There are many things that account for it but the devil is behind it all. For one thing, people are tired. They have been so bewildered with the things that are happening that they are dizzy. They ran themselves out of breath trying to outrun the depression, and now they are breaking their necks trying to get all they can, until when they sit down at church they are exhausted. Then they have listened to so much from platform and pulpit and radio, read so much from papers and magazines, been preached at and preached to, lectured and electioneered, cussed and discussed, gypped and cheated and lied to, and have bought gold bricks and white elephants, until they come to church with their fingers crossed, ready to take what they hear with a grain of salt, and the preacher has two strikes against him before he utters a word. Besides all that, the devil has cocained and chloroformed this present age, until a strange coma has settled over the saints, as well as the sinners, and our eyelids are heavy and our brains are clouded, and unless we stir up the gift of God within us and get down to business watching and praying, our Lord shall come suddenly and find us sound asleep.

We need to bestir ourselves and keep on the firing line for God, so that when our Lord comes we shall not be engaged in SCOFFING or SURFEITING or SLEEPING, but SERVING; not merely occupied with His coming, but occupying till He come. We want to be found "in him" (Phil. 3: 9), found watching (1 Thess. 5: 6), found in peace (2 Pet. 3: 14), found faithful (1 Cor. 4: 2). I am afraid that there is a sort of theoretical interest in the Lord's return prevalent among the saints that somehow does not seem to get hitched up to practical service. Some of the brethren are SIGHING over the times and wondering what we are coming to, but that is poor business for a Christian, who ought to know what we are coming to and be joyfully looking for his Lord to come. Others are STUDY-ING about it, and can give you remarkable explanations of the order of events and the meaning of 666 in Revelation, but, somehow, it is just a hobby that doesn't translate itself into action. Again, some of the saints are SINGING about the second coming, but it is one thing just to sing the national anthem during the war and quite another to go into battle. The best evidence that the Lord's return has really gotten hold of us is when we occupy till He come, do business for God, buy up the opportunities, because the days are evil.

The watchman in our text adds, "IF YE WILL EN-QUIRE, ENQUIRE YE: RETURN, COME." The need of the hour is a return to God, first of all on the part of God's people. And we need a watchman, a prophet, to call them to repentance. I have studied a lot about what ails the church today, I have prayed and watched and read and listened and tried to get my finger on the pulse of our spiritual life today the best way I know how, and I have come to the conclusion that one of our serious troubles is this: we have ignored and neglected and sometimes condemned one of the gifts of Christ to the church, the NEW TESTA-MENT PROPHET. I read, "And he gave some, apostles; and some, prophets; and some, evangelists; and some, pastors and teachers; for the perfecting of the saints, for the work of the ministry, for the edifying of the body of Christ"

[16]

(Eph. 4: 11, 12). When we use the word "prophet," we usually think of some of the Old Testament worthies, Elijah or Isaiah or Amos, or else we think of some prophecy expert predicting the end of all things. But a prophet has a work as distinctive and important as an evangelist or pastor or teacher. The list begins with "apostles," who were eye-witnesses of the resurrection, and who included Paul and Barnabas as especially designated by Christ and the Spirit. Of course, there are no apostles in that sense now. There are some who speak of this man or that as "an apostle of righteousness," for instance, but that is a general term for a man sent on a special mission. But there are still prophets whose business is to speak to edification, exhortation, and comfort (1 Cor. 14: 3), that is, to strengthen, stir, and soothe the saints. His work may remind you of a teacher in his edification, of an evangelist in his exhortation, and of a pastor in his comfort, but he is neither. He is a prophet whose ministry is not so much explanation as application, who stands in the gap and calls God's people back to the Lord. He does not predict the future, he gives out what God has already predicted in His Word. He is not a fore-teller but a forthteller, a voice in the wilderness, a watchman on the tower, a watchdog over the flock.

And notice that he comes ahead of evangelist, teacher, and pastor. And right there we uncover one of our troubles in the church today. We are trying to do the work of the evangelist, teacher, and pastor, when we need first a prophet to call the saints to confession and conversion. Evangelism is important, but it follows revival, and we have sidestepped revival in favor of teaching the saints, with occasional appeals to the sinners. The prophet needs to go ahead and stir up the church and call men to break up their fallow ground and prepare their own hearts. When the lost joy of salvation is restored to Christians, then will transgressors be taught God's ways and sinners be converted. After the prophet, the evangelist can reap the harvest among the lost; and then the teacher can teach the converts, and the pastor can shepherd them. But we have put the cart before the horse, and we have passed up the prophet and used the term only as a general designation of a preacher when God gave him a peculiar job as definite as teaching or the pastorate.

There is a reason behind all this. Christians do not like to have their sins exposed, and church officials do not like to have Nathan pointing a finger at them saying, " Thou art the man." Churches do not like to have their ailments diagnosed, they like to be let alone at ease in Zion, while the preacher either tickles their ears with a pleasant sermon or goes after the unconverted, who are not even there. They say the sins of the church should not be exposed to the world. Don't worry, the world has discovered them long ago! Denominations resent the prophet's call to repentance because sometimes he has to point out denominational sins that ought to be confessed, and they say he is not " loyal."

So prophets are not wanted, and therefore they are scarce, for few there be who will take up such a thankless ministry. People will go out to hear an evangelist or a teacher or a pastor, but they never fall over each other going to hear prophets. Prophets have been unpopular from the very beginning. God told Isaiah and Ezekiel that people would not heed their message. Jesus accused His people of persecuting the prophets of the past, and Stephen asked, " Which of the prophets have not your fathers persecuted? " (Acts 7: 52). We are told to covet the prophetic gift (1 Cor. 14: 39), but there are few candidates for it today, partly because it has been scandalized by false prophets but more because people don't like prophets, at least until after they are dead. The prophet usually is stoned while he lives, but another generation gathers up the stones and builds a monument in his honor.

But we shall never see a real awakening until the prophet

is recognized and until the church repents. Our Lord's last word to the church was not the Great Commission, but a call to repentance, over in Revelation. Ephesus has left her first love, and, according to our Lord's own words, she must REMEMBER whence she has fallen and REPENT and RE-DO—do again the first works, the works she started out doing and the works she started out to do.

We are talking evangelism and adding numbers to our churches before the churches are fit to receive new members. We are listening to Bible teaching, with sin complacently covered up in our lives. Pastors are wringing their hands over conditions in their churches, when, perhaps, they should turn prophet for the time being, or call in some brother who is a prophet, if such can be found. The time is come that judgment—self-judgment—should begin at the house of God before the fires of corrective judgment, which must begin at the house of God, break in all their fury. Away with all this armchair speculative study of prophecy that does not bring us to our knees! Away with this defeatist doctrine that there can never be another revival! It is an alibi to cover our sins, and " he that covereth his sins shall not prosper: but whoso confesseth and forsaketh them shall have mercy " (Prov. 28: 13). Let us hear the prophet of old, " IF YE WILL ENQUIRE, ENQUIRE YE, RETURN, COME." Get back to God in your hearts and in your homes and in your churches. Do not be satisfied to sing every Sunday morning, " There SHALL BE showers of blessing." If the showers do not come, it is a hollow mockery. God is not to blame. There CAN BE showers of blessing; there MUST BE; there WILL BE when we mean business and get right with God!

II

IT IS TIME FOR GOD TO WORK; IT IS TIME TO SEEK THE LORD

"It is time for thee, Lord, to work: for they have made void thy law."—PSALM 119: 126.

"Sow to yourselves in righteousness, reap in mercy: break up your fallow ground: for it is time to seek the Lord, till he come and rain righteousness upon you."—HOSEA 10: 12.

YOU will notice that in both these verses we have the phrase, "It is time." It is a common phrase of everyday speech. We are frequently saying, "It is time this happened," "It is time that took place."

In these two texts are suggested both God's sovereignty and human responsibility. "It is time for thee, Lord, to work"—that is God's business. "It is time to seek the Lord"—that is our business, and we had better be about it. "It is time for thee, Lord, to work." The situation to-day is ripe for revival. World conditions are absolutely hopeless unless God intervenes. The pendulum has swung about as far as it can in one direction. We face the Lord's return or revival or ruin. Yet in times so dire and dismal and desolate and desperate, Christians sit at ease in Zion, unawakened to the urgency and emergency of the age. I have often thought that the most unappreciated man is a Pullman porter, who has to go down that mahogany lane early in the morning to awaken passengers who are in no mood to be aroused. But this business of waking people up is a thankless job wherever you find it, whether it be that of a Pullman porter at 6 A. M. or a preacher's on Sunday at 11 A. M. There are those who come to the house of God across whose faces one can almost read that sign of hotel-room doors, "Please Do Not Disturb."

When someone in the home is sick, we think nothing of sitting up all night. We change the schedule of the entire household to meet the emergency. When catastrophe strikes a community, radio programs are brushed aside, railroad schedules may be disrupted, and the whole set-up is adjusted to suit the situation. Yet we live in a world sick unto death in body, mind and spirit, fast approaching the end of the age, with more happening now in a day than used to happen in a month. Pity the poor fellow who lectures on current events! By the time he prepares his speech and delivers it, it sounds like ancient history! Yet in such an hour, instead of manning the lifeboats to save men from disaster, the saints make daisy chains and mud pies and piddle around on the brink of ruin. And the faithful preacher who would arouse the believers is sneered at by sanctuary slumberers, who want only " a little more sleep, a little more folding of the hands to sleep."

However we may disagree in interpreting the parable of the ten virgins, one feature of it is evident to anybody who will look around almost anywhere today: " While the bridegroom tarried, they all slumbered and slept." Truly, " it is high time to awake out of sleep " and " it is time for God to work."

Why is it time for God to work? " For they have made void thy law." If Paul could say in his day, " The mystery of lawlessness doth already work," what would he say today? There is a breakdown of authority everywhere. In the home, someone has said, there is as much authority as ever, but the children use it! Marriage has become a temporary arrangement instead of a permanent partnership. The officer of the law is a joke to many and dodging the law is a popular pastime. Anarchy is evident in all fields. Consider art, for instance. Have you paid much attention to a surrealistic picture? Did you know what you were seeing? You cannot tell whether it is a sunset or scrambled eggs. I have heard that one was hung upside down in an exhibit recently and that it won the prize, nobody knowing the difference. It is simply anarchy in art. Swing music is music without authority, music gone crazy. Then there is international lawlessness. For further information read your newspaper!

The churches have made void God's law. Authority has disappeared from pulpits, where religious dishwater, perfumed with ethical lavender, is being sprayed over the sins of an ungodly world. Our Lord spake as having authority, and we are bidden to speak, exhort, rebuke with all authority, as the oracles of God. Alas, too many of us are described by the colored minister down South who got mixed up in introducing another minister and said, " Our brother is well reversed in the Scriptures! " We lack the note of " Thus saith the Lord."

The professing church has made void God's law. Having begun in the Spirit, too often has she sought to make herself perfect in the flesh. Teaching and financial and social programs have been borrowed from the world. The early Christians went out " taking nothing from the Gentiles." Now we take all we can get. David hauls the ark on a new cart. The spirit of the shop has invaded the sanctuary. Preachers' studies have become offices. Corporation methods have taken the place of consecrated men. Human busyness has supplanted the Father's business. We are running around in our sleep, knocking things over and calling it " Kingdom work." We have made void God's law of Pentecost, so we have pandemonium.

We Christians have made void God's law. We have become a law unto ourselves instead of fulfilling the law of Christ. We have made void the law of Philippians 1: 21 and Galatians 2: 20 and the eighth chapter of Romans. If some could even get into the seventh of Romans and become miserable over their state, there might be hope for revival!

[22]

Truly, we have made void God's law and it is time for God to work. But it is also time to seek the Lord, as our other text tells us. He has said, " Ye shall seek me and find me when ye shall search for me with all your heart " (Jer. 29: 13). Our God is the Rewarder of them that diligently seek Him, but we must be diligent, in dead earnest. It is knee-time in America, and, no matter how crowded our schedule, we had better put at the top of it, " It is time to seek the Lord."

Now, Hosea tells us very practically how we are to seek the Lord: " Break up your fallow ground: for it is time to seek the Lord, till he come and rain righteousness upon you." If the Lord is to rain righteousnes, we must prepare the soil of our hearts. We sing in our churches:

> " There shall be showers of blessing:
> This is the promise of love;
> There shall be seasons refreshing,
> Sent from the Saviour above.
> There shall be showers of blessing,
> Precious reviving again;
> Over the hills and the valleys,
> Sound of abundance of rain."

But, for all our singing, the revival has not come. Some of us are growing embarrassed about it. We have talked so much about revival that the world is beginning to ask, " But where are the showers of blessing? " The trouble is indicated in our text. We have never broken up the fallow ground of our cold hearts, and God will not waste His rain on briars and thorns! Fallow ground is UNPRODUCTIVE BECAUSE IT IS UNDISTURBED. And just so the hearts of Christians, unless they are stirred with the plow of conviction and brought to repentance, grow hard and become covered with weeds and thorns. We must prepare the soil before God will send rain. It is true that God gives the increase, but we have to do some farming. No farmer can ever raise a crop until he disturbs the soil, and it is just as foolish for Christians to pray for revival showers without breaking up their hearts.

We must investigate ourselves and take stock and make an inventory and put in the plow and break up the soil and tear up roots of bitterness and present to God a broken and contrite heart. Pride must be confessed, restitution made, criticism acknowledged, grudges forgiven, unlove removed, the wedge of gold uncovered. "Break up your fallow ground and sow not among thorns" (Jer. 4: 3). If you have not had a revival lately, is it not because your heart is cold and unconcerned? We have been complacent so long that to break up our hearts would seem like a major operation. Besides, it takes effort to break up fallow ground and we do not like to exert ourselves. "He that covereth his sins shall not prosper; but whoso confesseth and forsaketh them shall have mercy" (Prov. 28: 13).

Christmas Evans, the great Welsh preacher, relates that he was riding on horseback through the mountains one Saturday on his way to preach, when he became convicted of a cold heart. He tethered his horse and spent about four hours in soul-searching and prayer before God. His soul was revived with a joyous experience, like the "breaking up of a hard winter," and he went on his way to preach on Sunday, with the result that a gracious revival began and spread over all the community.

Surely we need something like "the breaking up of a hard winter" in our hearts today. Will you confess that your heart is fallow? Will you acknowledge and forsake the sin that God points out in your heart? If you do not feel like repenting, will you confess that and ask God to help you to do what you ought to do, whether you feel like it or not?

Let us get back to God's time-table: "It is time for God to work. . . . It is time to seek the Lord."

III

TIME FOR JUDGMENT

"For the time is come that judgment must begin at the house of God: and if it first begin at us, what shall the end be of them that obey not the Gospel of God? And if the righteous scarcely be saved, where shall the ungodly and the sinner appear?"—I PETER 4: 17, 18.

PETER wrote his letters to Christians in a day of testing and suffering to build them up for greater trials yet to come. In these troubled days, when Christians think it strange concerning the fiery trial which is testing so many of the saints, we do well to fortify ourselves with these words from the great apostle.

When I read this text, my mind goes back to the days of Ezekiel. He was another great preacher living in captivity in a sad and bewildering day. In the eighth and ninth chapters of his book, we read that God gave him a vision, turning time backward in its flight and carrying Ezekiel to show him the reason why Israel was now captive in Babylon. In this retrospective revelation, God showed him through a hole in the wall the elders engaging in idolatry, women giving themselves to phallic cults, and men worshipping the sun. It was as though God said to the prophet, " Ezekiel, when the young generation now growing up in exile wants to know why I allowed my chosen people to go into captivity, these chapters from the past will explain it. It is righteous judgment for their sin."

Then, in the ninth chapter, six men come forth, and a man with a writer's inkhorn by his side is sent out to mark all who are burdened for the sins of the people. Then the men with weapons are sent after him to kill all that are not marked, and they are told, " BEGIN AT MY SANCTUARY." So here judgment begins at the house of God.

Surely we live today in an age that bears all the marks of the days of Ezekiel. Idolatry, phallic cults and sun-worship have nothing on America. We can match the filthiest corruptions which Ezekiel saw any day and we don't have to look through a hole in the wall to see them. Recently I read of a party staged in a great city where each one who attended came representing a certain god. One came representing God Almighty, and another posed as the leading curse word in America that uses the name of God. When I read that, I reflected that since one of Satan's first words to man was, " Ye shall be as gods," and since Anti-christ will claim to be God, we are certainly running true to form.

The man with the writer's inkhorn was to mark all who were burdened over the sins of the people and all others were to be slain. If that procedure were followed in America, no massacre in history could compare with it, for few there be who care that we have forsaken God. Amos lamented in his day that no one was grieved for the affliction of Joseph. Jeremiah asked, " Is it nothing to you, all ye that pass by? " In the days of Malachi the people met his condemnation of sin with a cynical " Wherein? " Isaiah lamented that he dwelt among a people of unclean lips. Paul could wish himself accursed for the sake of his brethren. Moses asked to be blotted out of God's book for the sake of Israel. Our Lord was grieved over Jerusalem. We need today the spirit of a Knox crying, " God, give me Scotland or I die! " We need the heart of a Brainerd wrestling in prayer for the Indians. Not only do we not care for the souls of sinners, alas, we care not for our own. The man with the writer's inkhorn would not be overworked today marking all Americans who are concerned on account of sin. He wouldn't need much ink to brand the burdened among us!

You will observe that one of the characteristics of Ezekiel's day was that the people kept saying, " The Lord seeth us not; the Lord hath forsaken the earth " (8: 12; 9: 9). In other words, " God doesn't care what we do; there is no wrath, no hell, no judgment." They said the same thing in Job's time: " It profiteth a man nothing that he should delight himself with God " (34: 9). They said it to Jeremiah: " Where is the Word of the Lord? Let it come now " (17: 15). They said it to Malachi: " Where is the God of judgment? " (2: 17). We hear it everywhere today: " God doesn't care: if He did, there would not be such misery and bloodshed. Therefore, it doesn't matter how we live."

God has a striking figure in the Old Testament to describe human hearts that have grown indifferent to God. In Zephaniah we read: " And it shall come to pass at that time that I will search Jerusalem with candles and punish the men that are SETTLED ON THEIR LEES, that say, the Lord will do no good, neither will he do evil " (1: 12). And Jeremiah says of the Moabites: " Moab hath been at ease from his youth and he hath SETTLED ON HIS LEES and hath not been emptied from vessel to vessel; neither hath he gone into captivity; therefore his taste remained in him and his scent is not changed " (48: 11).

The figure " settled on their lees " is that of vinegar, for instance, that has been allowed to set until a scum has formed over it; or of milk that has turned to curds. It describes the same spiritual state as " resting at ease in Zion " ; it is the lukewarm state of the Laodiceans. And it is the condition, not only of sinners, but of thousands of Christians today. Our churches have settled on their lees. They have been let alone so long, they have been undisturbed by real conviction and repentance, until a scum has gathered over the saints. It is disastrous to be let alone too long. God has a way of shaking up His saints. He pours them from vessel to vessel to prevent their turning to curds. Sometimes sickness will stir them up. Financial reverses, even a death in the family, may be necessary. If we judged ourselves, we should not be judged, but we settle on our lees and God has to jolt and jar us loose. That is why we need revivals. A good old revival is always a blessing because it pours the saints into a new vessel. I know that revival should be the normal state of the church, but it is not, and therefore we need a good shaking up now and then to prevent a spiritual scum from gathering. We need bombshell sermons and pulpit dynamite to blast the sanctuaries out of dead formalism. "It is high time to awake out of sleep," and, however much they may resent it, better disturb the Sunday-morning sanctuary sleepers and empty them from vessel to vessel than let them come to judgment settled on their lees. If some object that revivals are temporary, better remember Billy Sunday's word: "So is a bath, but it does you good!" God is not always emptying the saints from vessel to vessel, but they need it once in a while. Too many sermons are bedtime stories to lull the saints to sleep instead of morning reveilles to wake them up!

The men who carried weapons were to follow the man with the writer's inkhorn and kill everyone whom he had not marked and THEY WERE TO BEGIN AT THE SANCTUARY. Peter says, "For the time is come that judgment must begin at the house of God." God begins with His own people: judgment, like charity, begins at home. Much of the blame for world conditions lies at the door of the church. Our indifference, our neglect, our failure to cry out against iniquity have encouraged the devil. Unfaithful preachers, modernism, formality, worldliness, unholy living have disgraced the house of God until He must, like the Saviour of old, first cleanse the temple. God's house has become a den of thieves and it is time for the whip of judgment.

Two kinds of judgment appear in our text: CORRECTIVE JUDGMENT FOR THE SAINTS, CONDEMNATORY JUDGMENT FOR THE SINNERS. "If it first begin at us, what shall the end be of them that obey not the gospel of God? And if the righteous scarcely be saved, where shall the ungodly and the sinner appear? " " Behold, the righteous shall be recompensed in the earth: much more the wicked and the sinner " (Prov. 11: 31).

We are entering upon the last days and God is sifting His people. There is beginning right now a separation between the great crowd of Sunday-morning churchgoers and those who really mean business with God. On one hand, we have the mass of nominal Christians who belong to church because the family does or because it is the nice thing to do, who draw nigh to God with their mouths and honor Him with their lips, while their hearts are far from Him. These will soon be shown up in their true colors: they will trim their sails to catch the breeze and end up in one great apostate aggregation in league with the powers that be, the world, the flesh and the devil. On the other hand, is the faithful remnant who fear the Lord and speak often one to another, saints from all the church bodies, drawn together by a common love for Christ. These will be melted together in fires of testing with a comradeship like that of the early Christians in the catacombs of Rome. For although saints now living will not go through the final Great Tribulation, if our Lord tarries, many of them may see great tribulation. Judgment is beginning today at the house of God and we shall see who is who in the days ahead.

Peter says, " If the righteous scarcely be saved——" So severe will be the testing that even true Christians barely will be saved. There will be times when it will seem that God has forsaken us, nights so dark that no star will appear. Men's faith will be strained almost to the breaking point. The strongest saints will tremble and the stoutest hearts will faint. No wonder that Peter adds: " Wherefore let them that suffer according to the will of God commit the keeping of their souls to him as unto a faithful creator."

It has not cost much lately to be a Christian. We sit in comfortable churches singing:

> " To the old rugged cross I will ever be true,
> Its shame and reproach gladly bear."

But we have not realized what we were singing. That shame and reproach will be an actual experience, and when persecution arises because of the Word, many will be offended. A Lutheran tract quotes a pastor as saying:

" All kinds of strange feelings and new and peculiar trials will come to us. A surprising lack of desire and energy Godward, a spiritual deadness, a mental heaviness, lethargy of soul, an alarming desire for forbidden things and a peculiar delight and fascination in any of the world's pleasures we dare taste. It will be difficult to preach the Word in liberty and power; it will be difficult to give attention to the Word when it is preached; it will be very difficult to get down to real earnest and continued prayer."

The sifting of the saints is going on right now before our eyes. There are great church movements and drives and programs that stage impressive mass demonstrations, but it is to be questioned how much of them is owned and operated by the Spirit of God. God's movement today is a deeper urge among believers in all church bodies who are returning to the Word of God and the old-time testimony. Unanimity they will never have, for that is not essential; unification they do not want, for that is man-made; but unity of the Spirit binds them together, for they gather around one Lord. It is a mark of the end of the age, for God is gathering His own from all the churches, not by movements engineered by men, but by a common love for Christ that shines more brightly as the days grow darker.

Indeed, right here is a remarkable thing about this unity

of the saints in these last days. This drawing together is a work of the Spirit, but when we try to do it we fail. This union of Bible Christians does not lend itself to our systems and plans, and when some man tries to head it up or put a tag on it, he fails, but the movement goes right on. We would do better to exalt Christ and preach the Word and not try to engineer the work of the Spirit too closely.

Truly, the time has come that judgment has begun at the house of God, and the best advice I can give is found in the first part of this same chapter from First Peter. There is an Old Testament exhortation, " Sanctify yourselves against tomorrow." It is a timely word now. If you are a lukewarm Christian, out of fellowship and out of tune with God, I beseech you, set your house in order, for the storm is upon us and even the righteous will scarcely be saved. Return to God, confess your sin, claim the cleansing blood. Get back to the Book and watch unto prayer. Straighten out your affairs with your fellow men. See that you have a conscience void of offense toward God and man. Commit your soul to God, rest in the Rock of Ages, where neither bombs nor blackouts can disturb. Learn the joy of abiding in the cleft of the Rock and learn how to sing:

> " When peace like a river attendeth my way;
> When sorrows like sea-billows roll;
> Whatever my lot, Thou hast taught me to say,
> It is well, it is well, with my soul."

One other serious consideration claims our attention. If this judgment begin at us, " what shall the end be of them that obey not the Gospel of God? And if the righteous scarcely be saved, where shall the ungodly and the sinner appear? " Truly, " the ungodly shall not stand in the judgment nor sinners in the congregation of the righteous." If these lines fall under the eye of an unsaved reader, let me warn you to flee from the wrath to come. Do not make lies your refuge, nor under falsehood hide yourself. Do not say, " I have made a covenant with death, and with hell I am at agreement." If the saints scarcely be saved in their corrective judgment, what will you do in the judgment of condemnation? You will cry for rocks and mountains to fall on you, to hide you from the face of Christ the Judge. He Himself said, " Whosoever shall fall on this stone shall be broken; but on whomsoever it shall fall, it will grind him to powder " (Matt. 21: 44). He is now the Rock of Refuge, " Rock of Ages, cleft for me." One day He will be the Rock of Judgment. And if you do not fall on the Rock, the Rock will one day fall on you. If you do not fall upon Him in repentance, He will fall upon you in judgment. You cannot hide from God. " He that covereth his sins shall not prosper: but whoso confesseth and forsaketh them shall have mercy " (Prov. 28: 13). This judgment is upon them that obey not the Gospel. What is it to obey the Gospel? " Believe on the Lord Jesus Christ and thou shalt be saved." " He that believeth is not condemned." Trust Him, commit all you are and have to Him, and when the storm of judgment breaks, you will have a hiding place, having committed the keeping of your soul to Him in well-doing as unto a faithful Creator.

IV

TIME TO WAKE UP

"And that, knowing the time, that now it is high time to awake out of sleep: for now is our salvation nearer than when we believed. The night is far spent, the day is at hand: let us therefore cast off the works of darkness, and let us put on the armor of light. Let us walk honestly, as in the day; not in rioting and drunkenness, not in chambering and wantonness, not in strife and envying. But put ye on the Lord Jesus Christ, and make not provision for the flesh, to fulfill the lusts thereof."—ROMANS 13: 11–14.

WE are living in the Saturday evening of the age. As it was in the days of Noah so it is today. The "perilous times" have come. Iniquity abounds, and while the love of many should wax hot, the Bible says it shall wax cold and so it has. The night of apostasy deepens. The mystery of lawlessness heads toward its awful climax. The maps of the world change overnight. The nations are being shuffled on the checkerboard of time and the stage is rapidly being set for the final act in the drama of the ages.

Not long ago a fellow passenger said to me as we sat at dinner on a train discussing current happenings, "If somebody had written all these things in a book, no one would have believed it." I replied, "That is just it: much of it has been written in a Book, and very few believe it."

Someone has said that America is a wilderness without a voice. It would be better to say that it is a wilderness with too many voices. We have been listening to professors and philosophers; we need a prophet. But prophets are unpopular today, not only in their own country, but in any country. They get bricks while they live and bouquets after they die. One generation kills them and the next builds tombs for them and garnishes their sepulchers.

[33]

The need of the hour is a prophet's call to repentance and a return to God. Certainly the church needs to remember that our Lord's last recorded message to the saints is not the Great Commission but His call to repentance to five churches out of seven in Revelation.

The professing church may be divided into three groups. First, there are the modernists. Modernism has no message, for it denies the only hope of the world, a supernatural Bible and a supernatural Christ. It is rooted in evolution and therefore rotten at the source. It denies the depravity of the human heart and the need of a blood-bought redemption. It laughs at a " slaughter-house theology " and eliminates the blood songs from our hymnals. It takes the precious name of our Lord, " Emmanuel," and removes the " Em " from the beginning and the " uel " from the ending and leaves only " man," forgetting that " no mortal can with Him compare among the sons of men." It calls weakness what God calls wickedness, recommends culture instead of Calvary and polish instead of pardon. It has tried to revise the Bible, streamline the Gospel, remodel heaven, explain away the devil, and air-condition hell. It has no hallelujah. It never produced a revival. It never saved a soul. It never convicted a sinner. It never changed a dope fiend into a disciple. It never transformed a criminal into a Christian. It never took away a drunkard's love for boots or loosed a libertine from the shackles of lust. It is a form without force, a religion without redemption. It defies the Book, denies the blood and derides the blessed hope, and the wrath of God abides upon it.

Then we have the denominationalists. We have no sympathy with those who are reluctant to disclose their denominational affiliation. If I were ashamed of my church connection I would join another. One may be ashamed of what some do in his denomination without being ashamed of what it really stands for. Many denominations might be better if we cried out against their evils instead of looking the other way and pretending that they do not exist.

Nor do we have any sympathy with those who would lump all the major church bodies into one apostate aggregation and dump them bodily into perdition. Granting that the great church groups will end up finally in an apostate world church, they have not done so yet, and there is as much godliness in some of them as in some disgruntled groups, who remind us of those matches that won't strike on any box except their own!

But, on the other hand, it is not likely that the next revival will come through the great church bodies officially. There is much being said about evangelism, but very little about revival. There is too much ecclesiasticism and modernism and worldliness and catering to the spirit of the times. Roger Babson well said, " Our churches will never get to first base by imitating popular service luncheon clubs." The person of Christ is easily lost in a program about Him. We have emphasized programs and propaganda and pep and personnel, when we need most passion and power. We are trying to make church members do a lot of things they don't want to do anyway. When the love of God is shed abroad in our hearts, it will not be necessary to encourage the saints by prizes and picnics and periodic shots in the arm to do the will of God. Churches, like Samson, have gone to sleep in the lap of Delilah, and though they go forth Sunday after Sunday to shake themselves, the Spirit of the Lord has departed. Samson may have looked better after he had his hair cut, but he lost his power. The world, the flesh and the devil have given the churches a hair cut. We have renounced our separation and have become conformed instead of transformed. And unless there is repentance and humbling before God and confession of sin from top to bottom in our major church bodies, God may use some irregular means as He has done before to call men back to Him. Peter Waldo and the poor men of Lyons, Wickliffe and the Lollards, Fox and the Friends, Wesley and the lay preachers, Moody and Billy Sunday—here are examples of God moving outside the conventional circles to carry on His work when the churches officially go to sleep.

Then we have the fundamentalists. Unfortunately, the name " fundamentalist," if it does not cover a multitude of sins, certainly does cover a multitude of schisms. So many cliques have sprung up that a suitable greeting would be, " How are you clique-ing? " The New Testament tells of Demas, who loved this present world; Diotrephes, who loved the pre-eminence; and Demetrius, who loved the truth. Bible believers might well be classified by these three D's.

But we do thank God for all who believe and preach the old-time religion in a time like this. Particularly do we owe it to the fundamentalists that they have recovered and re-sounded the precious message of the Lord's return. It is that blessed hope that is set before us in our text: " NOW IS OUR SALVATION NEARER THAN WHEN WE BELIEVED. THE NIGHT IS FAR SPENT, THE DAY IS AT HAND." Well did G. Campbell Morgan say:

" To me the second coming is the perpetual light on the path which makes the present bearable. I never lay my head on the pillow without thinking that perhaps before the morning breaks, the final morning may have dawned. I never begin my work without thinking that He may inter-rupt my work and begin His own. This is now His word to all believing souls, ' Till I come.' We are not looking for death, we are looking for Him."

Spurgeon said, " Apart from the second advent of our Lord, the world is more likely to sink into a pandemonium than to rise into a millennium." How anyone can stand with an open Bible in one hand and a newspaper in the other and believe otherwise can be explained only by the words of Holy

Writ, " For this they WILLINGLY are ignorant of "
(2 Pet. 3: 5).

Yet one encounters some strange reactions to this precious truth, even among those who hold it. There are the defeatists, who reason that, since we are in the great apostasy, there can never be another awakening. So they sit with hands folded in pious resignation, snug and smug in their orthodoxy, occupied with His coming but not occupying till He come. It is fine to know prophetic truth but it carries with it serious responsibility. " Unto whomsoever much is given, of him shall be much required." Prophetic doctrine brings with it personal duty: " Seeing then, that all these things shall be dissolved, what manner of persons ought ye to be? " The blessed hope should be accompanied by blessed holiness, for he that truly hath this hope in him purifieth himself.

It is strange that some should make prophetic truth to discourage revival. There is no greater incentive to revival than the hope of our Lord's return. Revival grows out of a knowledge of the times in our text: " AND THAT, KNOWING THE TIME, THAT NOW IT IS HIGH TIME TO AWAKE OUT OF SLEEP." What is revival but the saints awaking out of sleep? One of America's great revivals was called The Great Awakening. Instead of concluding that, since we are in the last days, there is no use expecting a mighty awakening, that very fact should fire us to renew the covenant, go back to Bethel, set our house in order and sanctify ourselves against tomorrow!

With this background of the times, Paul exhorts us with a call to duty: " THE NIGHT IS FAR SPENT, THE DAY IS AT HAND: LET US THEREFORE . . ." Then follow three sets of admonitions, both positive and negative. " Let us therefore cast off the works of darkness, and let us put on the armor of light." Here is something to put off and something to put on. One might as well try to wear

[37]

two suits at once as to try the armor of light without shedding the works of darkness.

"Let us walk honestly, as in the day . . ." Here is the positive followed by three sets of negatives: "not in rioting and drunkenness, not in chambering and wantonness, not in strife and envying." Here God rates strife and envying along with downright immorality and sordid wickedness. Some who glory in their abstinence from the first four of these sins are past masters at the last two. A good text for more than one fundamental church would be, "Let there be no strife, I pray thee, between me and thee . . . for we be brethren" (Gen. 13:8). This verse reminds us of another, in which God classifies busybodies along with murderers, thieves and evildoers (1 Pet. 4:15). In the sight of God, Diotrephes loving the pre-eminence is as distasteful as Demas loving this present world. It has never dawned on some who boast of their separation that strife and envying are listed in the same category with the grievous vices they abhor. Sam Jones used to observe that when dogs fought over bones, it was a sign that bones were scarce; and that when men quarreled over religion, religion was scarce in the neighborhood.

But the climax of this passage is verse 14: "But put ye on the Lord Jesus Christ, and make not provision for the flesh, to fulfil the lusts thereof." Christ is the climax of the chapter and anything that does not find its climax in Him is anticlimax and anti-Christ.

This verse, which changed the life of Augustine, carries a positive and negative. We easily forget the negative, "Make not provision for the flesh." Sometimes we put on the Lord Jesus and make a profession of full consecration, then go out and make arrangements to sin. It reminds us of the boy who went in swimming against his father's orders. When his father found him, the boy said, "I didn't mean to go in." "But why did you have your bathing suit with you? " his father demanded, and the boy replied, " I brought that along in case I was tempted! "

" Put ye on the Lord Jesus Christ "—there is the heart of it all! The nation needs Christ! Some time ago, near Washington, a friend took me for a drive. Coming to a new bridge, he said, " While this bridge is new, the foundations are a hundred years old. The engineers decided that the foundations were better than they could build now, so they just put a new bridge on top! " Would that our national engineers could learn that " other foundation can no man lay than that is laid, which is Jesus Christ " (1 Cor. 3: 11).

Modernism needs Christ. It has denied Him, preaching the crystal Christ instead of the Calvary Christ, the paragon instead of the Propitiation.

Denominationalism needs Christ. Sometimes it loses Him in its very work for Him. Joseph and Mary lost Jesus in the temple, and He can be lost right in church. He that gathereth not WITH HIM scattereth abroad, and there is often much activity about and for Him which He does not own.

Fundamentalism needs Christ. Sometimes He may be in the head but not in the heart. It is possible to defend the miracles of yesterday and not know a miracle in one's own life today. One may spend a lifetime expounding the supernatural without experiencing it, protecting the truth without proving it.

We all need Christ. Orthodoxy is not enough. Activity is not enough. Separation from sin is not enough. " Put on the Lord Jesus Christ." Make sure that He is your Saviour through faith in Him. Make Him Lord of your life. Resign in His favor! Let Him increase and yourself decrease, until you truly can say, " Not I but Christ."

V

TIME TO BE SERIOUS

"But this I say, brethren, the time is short: it remaineth, that both they that have wives be as though they had none; and they that weep as though they wept not; and they that rejoice as though they rejoiced not; and they that buy as though they possessed not; and they that use this world, as not abusing it: for the fashion of this world passeth away."—1 Corinthians 7: 29–31.

THIS solemn statement of Paul sets forth our pattern of conduct in the last days. It begins and ends with a reminder of how short and changing are these fleeting times: " The time is short. . . . The fashion of this world passeth away." Of course, there is a sense in which the time has always been short. It was short in Paul's day for, compared with endless eternity, the whole stretch of history is less than a drop of water beside all the oceans. But now, with all the signs of the times fast converging and God's signals going off all around us, who can doubt that the sands of the age are running low? It is true that at every crisis of history there have always been some to prophesy that judgment was just around the corner. But their mistakes do not mean that we will not eventually reach that corner. Never have all the trends and tendencies and indications that mark the end of the age come together in such a pattern as we now behold. To go into that is not the purpose of this message, but humble students of the Word and the times are growing pretty unanimous that " the time is short."

Nothing is clearer in the Word of God than that in these last days Christians are called to unusual seriousness and special urgency, while they walk circumspectly, redeeming the time because the days are evil. Especially does the Word

exhort believers to " be sober." The bishop must be sober
(1 Tim. 3: 2). The deacons' wives must be sober (1 Tim.
3: 11). Soberness is enjoined upon aged men (Titus 2: 2),
young women (Titus 2: 4), and young men (Titus 2: 6).
We are to gird up the loins of our minds and be sober
(1 Pet. 1: 13), to think of ourselves soberly (Rom. 12: 3),
and to be sober and vigilant (1 Pet. 5: 8).

In the light of God's picture of the times, in the urgency
and emergency of a world hastening to disaster, surely, if
ever the church ought to live with loins girded and lamps
burning, praying and preaching with the light of another
world in her eyes, it is today. Over and over we are exhorted to awake, to watch and pray, to exhort one another,
and so much the more as we see the day approaching. It
was for such a time that Paul set forth in the words of the
text the urgency of the situation and our proper behavior
in it.

" It remaineth that . . . they that have wives be as
though they had none." Believers are not to be too much
taken up with domestic cares. Now the world gives too
little importance to marriage, as the divorce courts testify:
but some Christians make it too important, so that it becomes their whole life. It was a mark of Noah's day that
the people were marrying and giving in marriage (Matt.
24: 38), that is, such things were their life. In these last
days we are not to make home and family our supreme
concern.

Many Christians will not need this injunction, for they
do not even love their families enough. But others will need
to hear our Lord's word about hating father and mother, wife
and children, brethren and sisters, and even one's own life.
Evangelists and missionaries often have had to keep Paul's
word literally, but to the general Christian witness in the
last days it merely means that domestic interests shall not
be our prime concern. Of course, some crank will get the

text by the wrong handle and suppose that he is to turn celibate, but Paul assumed that the average reader would apply it with sanctified common sense.

" And they that weep as though they wept not." We are not to be too much taken up with our sorrows. We are to be " sorrowful, yet always rejoicing " (2 Cor. 6: 10). Concerning departed loved ones, we are not to sorrow as others who have no hope (1 Thess. 4: 13). We are not to nurse old heartaches, mistakes and bereavements, living in the past beside the casket of the dead in the graveyard of yesterday. Forgetting the things that are behind, we are to let the dead bury their dead. God said to Joshua: " Moses my servant is dead; now therefore, arise, go over this Jordan " (Josh. 1: 2). The time is too short to spend it with our sorrows. It is not a cold, hard stoicism that is set before us here. Rather, Jesus is coming! There is too much to do to be occupied with our own troubles.

" And they that rejoice as though they rejoiced not." We are not to be too much taken up with our joys. We are to sit loose to our enjoyments and not to be so occupied, even with wholesome pastimes and recreations, that we cannot do without them. Ministers whose golf score is better than their prayer score may well take heed! We must be moderate even in our mirth, for such things are not our chief portion. Our joy is in the Lord, and it is easy to let the good endanger the best. If Satan cannot entrap us in our sorrows he will ensnare us with our joys.

In times of great crisis ordinary mirth is quite out of place. God's alarm clock is going off every hour nowadays, and Christians should not be content with conduct which ordinarily would have been sufficient in times past. These are no ordinary times and ordinary conduct is unbecoming! During floods, earthquakes, wars, people forego ordinary comforts, revise all their habits, and do things they never would do in ordinary times. If these temporal things stir men to unusual conduct, how much more should the people of God arouse themselves in these fearful days with unutterable judgment fast approaching! This is no time for trivial, silly banter and the small talk with which men come even to the doors of the church on the Lord's Day and which they resume as soon as they go out. Listening to us Christians around the church on Sunday morning, one would never suspect that the world was on fire, that Jesus was coming and that we were Christ's witnesses in the end of the age. Verily, some mistaken sects and isms put us to shame, standing on street corners in all kinds of weather, handing out their literature of error, while we live in a day of good tidings and hold our peace! We are so taken up with our little joys that the supreme joy is quenched within us.

"And they that buy as though they possessed not." It is not that we are to wear gunny-sack garments, for there is no holiness in a hair shirt, but we must be poor in spirit. What we possess must not possess us. Many are kept away from the Great Supper because of land and oxen. In the last days it shall be as in the days of Lot: "They did eat, they drank, they bought, they sold, they planted, they builded" (Lk. 17: 28). These things were their life and they must not be ours. This is no time for believers to hang up their stockings for the Santa Claus of this age to fill. It is no time to feather our nest with earthly comforts. Someone has said, "Not wanting a thing is comparable to possessing it." And even better than possessing many things is to be independent of them.

"And they that use this world, as not abusing it." It is the present world set-up that is in mind, the system which is so unmistakably under the prince of darkness. To be sure, we must have cars, clothes, money; we are not to hide in a cave (cf. 1 Cor. 5: 10). But these things are but a means to an end, and the traveler must not become absorbed in his baggage. " Give me neither poverty nor riches; feed me with food convenient for me. Lest I be full and deny thee and say, Who is the Lord? Or lest I be poor and steal and take the name of my God in vain " (Prov. 30: 8, 9). We are not glorifying poverty, for it is easy to fall into the Colossian error of a false mysticism, asceticism and neglecting of the body. It has been said: " Humility does not consist in thinking meanly of ourselves; it consists in not thinking of ourselves at all." " Having food and raiment, let us be therewith content " (1 Tim. 6: 8). " No man that warreth entangleth himself with the affairs of this life; that he may please him who hath chosen him to be a soldier " (2 Tim. 2: 4). " Love not the world, neither the things that are in the world " (1 John 2: 15). There are too many *de luxe* Christians who adopt a manner of living that poorly befits the way of the cross.

We are to use but not abuse. " Let your moderation be known unto all men. The Lord is at hand " (Phil. 4: 5). There is something a little ironical in a congregation of elegantly dressed Christians with jewels galore singing, " Take my silver and my gold, Not a mite would I withhold! " And it is a little amusing to watch a smug and comfortable crowd singing lustily, " A tent or a cottage, Why should I care? They're building a mansion for me over there! " This world is our passage and not our portion, but some of us drive our tent-pegs down as though we meant to stay.

" For the fashion of this world is passing away." It is not that it merely may pass or will pass, it is passing away right now before our eyes. " The world passeth away and the lust thereof " (1 John 2: 17). The old colored mammy who explained her tranquillity by saying, " I wear dis world lak a loose garment," was pretty near the truth of our text. And since the time is short and the fashion of this world passeth away and all these things shall be dissolved, what manner of persons ought we to be? "Let us who are of the day BE SOBER" (1 Thess. 5: 8).

There are boys selling newspapers and peddlers getting out their wares with more zeal than most of us ever rescue souls or preach the Word. A chaplain once asked his company just before they went into action, "Do you want me to conduct religious services or just tell you a good story?" and one soldier answered, "If you feel that way about it you might as well tell us a story." Some such flippant attitude is the mark of too many of us in this sad day. Life is too short and eternity is too long and souls are too precious and the Gospel is too wonderful for us to take it easy. Living in perilous times, in a crumbling civilization, with men's hearts failing them for fear, if ever God's people ought to live as "fools for Christ's sake," beside themselves and "drunk on new wine," as a peculiar people whose citizenship is in heaven, surely it is now. Let us be sober, for "the time is short" and "the fashion of this world passeth away."

VI

IT IS LATER THAN YOU THINK

SOMEWHERE I have read about a garden in which was a sundial bearing the inscription, " It Is Later Than You Think." In the wilderness of this world there is one sure sundial, the Word of God. From Genesis to Revelation it bears for us today the timely warning, " It Is Later Than You Think." In these frantic times, while millions rush madly through in modernity's much-ado-about-nothing, there are few who pause before the Eternal Time-piece to read its solemn message and meditate thereon.

To all of us comes its first warning: " It Is Later In The Age Than You Think." Writing to believers, Paul puts it thus: " For now is our salvation nearer than when we believed. The night is far spent, the day is at hand " (Rom. 13: 11, 12). We who believe in the second coming of our Lord as taught in the Word are not surprised that we should be unpopular with the scoffers of the latter days. We expect to be greeted in some quarters like poor relations come to town, as " representatives of a world view as hopeless as the contentions of the Guelphs and Ghibellines." When popular pulpits are fast agreeing with one of our philosophers that Christianity is " that body of myth and legend which is now passing from the theological to the literary stage (like the mythology of Greece and Rome in the medieval era)," we expect to be smiled out of some courts as cases of arrested development and nothing more.

But there are still thousands in this land who take their Bibles seriously—and all of them do not live in George Jean Nathan's " boll-weevil belt " either. As prophecy is rapidly fulfilled we do not exult in the gloating sense of the " I-told-you-so," for we are saddened that so many live through these days unready. But we do rejoice in the accuracy of the sundial of God's Word and we feel constrained to cry, "It is later than you think!"

If one listens only at random to the notes that sound from everywhere—from press or radio or ordinary conversation—it is the same story of a tower of Babel ending in confusion of tongues. Evolution has become devil-ution, the forces of the last world upheaval assemble, the sands of the age run low. Only the restraining hand of the Holy Spirit holds back the final flood of lawlessness. It is not law, the policemen, common morality, that does it. Armies policing the world will never do it. Yet men scorn the Gospel and blaspheme the Holy Spirit, not realizing that were it not for His restraining hand their very homes, children, jobs, property, lives would not be safe overnight.

A prominent liberal preacher admitted some years ago: "Neither Christian ministers nor anybody else may be able to do enough to save Western civilization from collapse. Surely our present civilization cannot survive and ought not to survive as it is." Then he would reassure us by saying: "Remember what Ralph Waldo Emerson said, that the lesson of life is to believe what the years and the centuries say against the hours." Well, in an entirely different sense we do believe in the testimony of the centuries against the hours. If we judged by the hours, there have been times when it looked as though men might fashion by their own wit and will an enduring Paradise. But when one sees the perspective of the ages from the viewpoint of the Word, he sees that God's eternal purpose rules otherwise. When man's last Utopia comes clattering down upon his head, God will bring in the Ideal Age in His own way. The hand of heaven is writing on the wall today. The soothsayers and astrologers are trying to read the signs with their usual success. God has numbered the kingdoms and finished them. We are weighed and found wanting. It is later than you think.

We pass on to a second truth: It is later in our lives than we think. "We spend our years as a tale that is told. The days of our years are threescore and ten; and if by reason of strength they be fourscore years, yet is their strength labor and sorrow: for it is soon cut off and we fly away" (Ps. 90: 9, 10). "For what is your life? It is even a vapour that appeareth for a little time and then vanisheth away" (Jas. 4: 14).

We have grown familiar with the proverbs about the brevity of life, and in many cases familiarity has bred contempt. A sophisticated generation smiles nonchalantly when the minister points out how short is our earthly pilgrimage. Many of them are finding life as they live it too long anyway. It has become smart to say that "life is only the predicament that precedes death," and, of course, the brevity of life means nothing if one believes that "youth is a blunder, maturity a struggle and old age a regret." In such a time it becomes increasingly difficult to impress upon cynical souls the value of these passing hours. But though today we see price instead of worth, God's standards have not changed. "To have is to owe, not own," and we must give account for the use of the years. Certainly, if ever we needed to number our days that we might apply our hearts unto wisdom, and if ever we needed to buy up the opportunities because the days are evil, it is today. And, contrary to popular notion, the younger we are, the more keenly we ought to feel that it is already later than we think. God would have us remember our Creator in the days of our youth, and there are things possible to youth that age, however earnest, can never know. Someone has said, "If only youth knew how to live and old age could! " How much truth is packed into that epigram, "Youth has fire without light and age has light without fire! " But by the grace of God youth may have Light to direct its fire and age may have Fire to warm its light. "Even the youths shall faint and be weary and the young men shall utterly fall: but they that wait upon the Lord shall renew their strength; they shall mount up with wings as eagles; they shall run and not be weary; and they shall walk, and not faint " (Isa. 40: 30, 31).

It is a tragic thing to end up one's days like Saul, trying to call back the Samuels of lost opportunity. There is no witch or wizard in time or eternity who can turn back time in its flight and make one " a child again just for tonight." I remember an old college professor who, every time he conducted chapel, used to remind us of that well-known advertisement, " Lost, one golden hour, studded with sixty diamond minutes; no reward offered, for it is gone forever." We used to smile at it, for he repeated it often; but, from the way some of those students turned out, it would have been better if they had listened instead of laughed. None of us can afford to piddle around with these passing days. It is later than you think.

Again, it is later in Christian opportunity than we think. Our Lord said, " I must work the works of him that sent me while it is day: the night cometh when no man can work " (John 9: 4). Dr. Samuel Johnson wore engraved on his watch the words, " The Night Cometh." We Christians ought to carry in our hearts the solemn truth of how short is our opportunity to witness for God among men. A dying Christian, who had been very reticent with his testimony all his life, said to Billy Bray, who sat beside him: " If I had the power I'd shout, Glory to God! " Billy replied, " It's a pity ye didn't shout Glory when ye had the power! " We had better be about our witnessing while we have the power.

Now is God's time for service, but many of us say by the way we live, " There are yet four months and then cometh harvest," when the fields are white today. We are disciples of the shade instead of the scythe. Dr. Thomas Chalmers tells of his awakening as a minister. He had been a mathematician all his life, he said, but he had overlooked the two greatest of magnitudes, the shortness of time and the vastness of eternity. There are some more of us who need to brush up on our spiritual mathematics!

> " Only one life, 'twill soon be past;
> Only what's done for Christ will last."

If we are to do better work for Christ we must know Him better, and now is the time for deeper fellowship with Him. How many of us, like the weary Emmaus disciples, need to pray, " Abide with us: for it is toward evening and the day is far spent " ! To be sure, He indwells the heart of the believer, but to so many He is not very real, because sin, indifference, doubt have hindered His manifestation in our hearts. We trust Him lamely, and though our hearts burn within us when we hear His words, there is a veiled communion and we need to realize His presence in our hearts and homes. It is toward evening with many of us and we need not trudge out our years in a pale and sickly experience. If we keep His commandments, trust and obey Him, He has promised to make Himself real (John 14: 21).

There is a precious verse in the Old Testament: " Sanctify yourselves against tomorrow " (Josh. 7: 13). We need to get ready today for tomorrow. First, there are the UNCERTAINTIES of tomorrow, we do not know what the next day holds. Some time ago I went to a home where a great tragedy had occurred, a fine son had drowned. But the parents were not caught off guard even by that. They did not need a lot of comfort, they had thatched the roof in dry weather, they had sanctified themselves against tomorrow, they were ready for whatever came. Again, there are the CERTAINTIES of tomorrow. We do know that death and judgment or the Lord's return must come on some tomorrow. And then there are the BLESSINGS of tomorrow. "Sanctify yourselves: for tomorrow the Lord will do wonders among you" (Josh. 3: 5). If we make the most of today there will be happy returns tomorrow.

Certainly, it is later than we think, and if ever we Christians are to witness, to know the Lord better, to glorify Him and help others, now is the time. "Exhort one another daily while it is called today" (Heb. 3: 13). Since the night is far spent and the day is at hand, let us cast off the works of darkness and put on the armor of light (Rom. 13: 12).

Finally, I could not close without seeking to impress upon the unsaved that it is later than you think. "Seek ye the Lord while he may be found, call ye upon him while he is near; let the wicked forsake his way, and the unrighteous man his thoughts: and let him return unto the Lord, and he will have mercy upon him; and to our God, for he will abundantly pardon" (Isa. 55: 6, 7). It is evident here that there will come a time when He will not pardon. "He that being often reproved hardeneth his neck shall suddenly be destroyed and that without remedy" (Prov. 29: 1). There can come a time when the harvest will be past, the summer ended, and you will not be saved. Now is the day of condemnation: "He that believeth not is condemned already" (John 3: 18), not at death, not at the judgment, but NOW. But NOW is also the day of salvation: "Behold, now is the accepted time; behold, now is the day of salvation" (2 Cor. 6: 2).

A woman, in view of an approaching lawsuit, planned to employ an able attorney in her town. After delay, she asked him to take her case. But it was too late. "I am very sorry," he said, "but I have just been appointed a judge. I cannot plead for you now, I can only judge you." The Lord Jesus is the believer's Advocate, but if you delay calling upon Him He must one day be your Judge.

" Tomorrow's sun may never rise
To bless thy long deluded sight;
THIS is the time, O then be wise;
O why not tonight? "

So many are lost because in youth they are " too young ";
in manhood, too busy; in maturity, too worried; when
aged, too old; when sick, too ill; and when dead, it is too
late. NOW is God's time. IT IS LATER THAN YOU
THINK!

VII

" LORD, DO IT AGAIN!"

THE prophet Isaiah was a faithful preacher in a nation going to pieces and headed for ruin. Sin abounded. God had been forgotten. False prophets were crying, " Peace," when there was no peace. The nation was trying to stave off disaster by making earthly alliances here and there, but Isaiah stood his ground and declared that all their schemes would crack up in defeat unless they turned to God. They called him a pessimist and a calamity howler, but when the enemy gathered at the gates of Jerusalem, King Hezekiah turned to the prophet of God, and when God was recognized, one hundred and eighty-five thousand Assyrian corpses were piled up by the angel of the Lord in one quick stroke of vengeance.

So it turned out that Isaiah was more than a prophet. He was not a politician running for something; he was a statesman who stood for something. He proved that one man and God make a majority. He was a living illustration of those immortal words of William Jennings Bryan in his " Cross of Gold " speech: " The humblest citizen of the land, when clad in the armor of a righteous cause, is stronger than all the hosts of error."

We need a prophet of his calibre and character and conviction in America today. We need to be reminded that our hope is not our allies but the Almighty. We need to learn that all our tanks and guns and planes may go down in defeat unless God come down to help us. We need to repent of taking the name of God in vain in our popular songs, of singing " God Bless America " when Americans are not ready to bless God, of trying to bolster morale with wine, women and song instead of learning to wait on the Lord and renew our strength. And when we do that, Hitler and Hirohito will be swept away like toothpicks before Niagara Falls, for although " careless seems the Great Avenger," yet " behind the dim unknown, standeth God within the shadows, keeping watch above His own."

In the sixty-fourth chapter of his book, Isaiah is looking around at the condition of the country. Then he looks back and remembers the days of old. He thinks of how God used to thunder at Sinai. He calls to mind the days of Moses and Joshua and Gideon and David, when Israel walked in power and the terror of the Lord went before them. Then he looks up and cries, " O that thou wouldest rend the heavens, that thou wouldest come down! " In other words, " O God, split the skies and come down again in mighty power as you used to do. Lord, DO IT AGAIN! "

We are living in a situation like that which Isaiah faced, except that it is a thousand times worse, for it is world-wide, and we need first to look AROUND as he did and size it up as it really is. We are hearing a lot of lovely oratory about the post-war world. Personally, I am unable to work up one bit of enthusiasm over this flood of eloquence, because not only are the speakers a thousand miles apart as to the world they are talking about, but they leave out the only ray of hope in the whole situation—a return to God. I need not dwell here on the fact that if we lose this war we are done for. But it is just as true that if we win it and leave God out, we are still done for.

Take the case of Europe alone. Those millions of people have been butchered and beaten until the survivors are be-side themselves. They have no money, no property, no homes, and they have been reduced to desperation until, if we won the war tomorrow, only God knows what demoniacal, demented anarchy would make the end of the other World War look like a picnic. There is no mortal man or group of men with one-millionth the wisdom it will take to unscramble this bloodcurdling mess. All eyes are on America, but we don't have what it takes. The only possible hope is the intervention of God. Therefore, like Isaiah, while we look AROUND, we need to look BACK at what God has done, and then we need to look UP and pray, " O that thou wouldest rend the heavens, that thou wouldest come down! Lord, DO IT AGAIN! "

For God has come down in the past and He will do it again. He came down in the Person of His Son to save us from our sins. He is coming again one of these days in the return of His Son to set up His kingdom. But between those two advents God has come down again and again in blessing upon His people. He came down at Pentecost. He has come down in gracious revivals. He made bare His mighty arm in Savonarola and Luther and Wesley and Whitefield and Finney, in the Great Awakening in early America, the Great Revival of 1800, the Welsh Revival not many years ago. He can do it again.

His resources are not limited. Look at verse 4: " For since the beginning of the world, men have not heard, nor perceived by the ear, neither hath the eye seen, O God, beside thee, what he hath prepared for him that waiteth for him." Paul quoted that in 1 Corinthians 2: 9, and he had in mind not only heaven but the riches of God's grace for us here and now. It is impossible to imagine, eye hath not seen, nor ear heard, what God can do to us and THROUGH us and FOR us when He can find a man who really cares enough to be His instrument. That is indicated in verse 5: " Thou meetest him that rejoiceth and worketh righteousness, those that remember thee in thy ways." God will meet any man more than halfway if that man is in dead earnest and means business with heaven. " The eyes of the Lord run to and fro throughout the whole earth, to show himself strong in the behalf of them whose heart is perfect toward him " (2 Chr. 16: 9).

Back in the 1600's God roused a serious-minded lad, so grieved over the sins of his time that he could not rest at ease in Zion but wandered in a leather suit all over England, calling men back to simple faith in God. He was George Fox, and he said, " The Lord had said unto me, If but one man or woman were raised up by His power to stand in the same spirit that the apostles and prophets were in, that man or woman would shake all the country for miles around." Two centuries later, a huge, rugged young Christian heard Henry Varley say, " The world has yet to see what God will do with and for and in and by the man who is fully consecrated to him," and then and there Dwight L. Moody resolved to be that man. The eyes of the Lord were running to and fro in the 1600's and found George Fox; in the 1800's they found Moody. Whom will they discover in the 1900's?

God is on the lookout for men and women who mean business with Him, who remember Him in all His ways, and He always meets such people in blessing and power. Long ago He found Savonarola so burdened over the sins of his day that he wrote:

> " Seeing the whole world overset,
>   All virtue and goodness disappeared;
>   Nowhere a shining light;
>   No man taking shame for his sins."

Maybe he overstated it, but, anyway, he was not wearing rose-colored glasses and painting the clouds with sunshine. And because he remembered God in His ways, God clothed him with power.

He found Jonathan Edwards, who said, " If it were revealed to me that in any stage of history there could be but one man who were in all to fulfil the will of God, I would strive with all my might to be that man "; and God gave him a message that made his listeners hang on to the pillars of the church before the terror of the Lord.

God looked around in Wales some years ago and found a serious-minded lad so burdened for revival that he lived in prayer that God might rend the heavens and come down— and God did come down in one of the mightiest revivals of history. Evan Roberts meant business and God met him.

God is on the lookout today for somebody who is concerned and in dead earnest about the state of his own heart and the need of the church and the world. He has blessed such people in the past with gracious revival. He can do it again.

It was after the funeral of General Booth of the Salvation Army, after the great congregation had left the church, that the sexton found one lone Methodist preacher on his knees at the altar. Moved with what God had wrought through the mighty life and work of William Booth, this solitary preacher was praying from the depth of his soul, " Lord, do it again! Lord, do it again! "

Yes, God can rend the heavens and come again in a mighty movement of His Spirit, and that is exactly what it will take to meet the need of this miserable hour in our hearts, our homes, our churches, our nation, our world. I mean more than a pleasant little Religious Retreat or a harmless Spiritual Emphasis Week. I mean more than a mere denominational drive or a much-advertised Preaching Mission. The times are too desperate for all that. We can do all these things and hold on to our sins, and right there is our trouble. Look at verses 5 and 6: " We have sinned. . . . We are all as an unclean thing and all our righteousnesses are as filthy rags." Our iniquities have separated us and our God. Our self-righteousness, like rags, does not cover us, but, like filthy rags, defiles us. We therefore need nothing less than a mourners-bench revival in the church of God that will bring His people down on their knees confessing and forsaking

[57]

their sins, for we cannot expect God to take away sin by forgiving it if we do not put it away by forsaking it; we need a revival that will empty theaters and fill churches and shut the mouths of critics and show this unbelieving world that what God has done He can do again.

Why should it be thought a strange thing to say that America's greatest need right now is a revival? This country was born and bred in revivals. Calvin Coolidge said, "America was born in a revival of religion. Back of that revival were John Wesley, George Whitefield and Francis Asbury." Our forefathers came over here out of a revival and the fires of faith in America have been kept burning all along by revivals, the Great Awakening, the Revival of 1800, the wave of revival started by the Fulton Street prayer meetings, the mighty movements of God through Moody and Torrey and Chapman and Sunday. President Franklin D. Roosevelt is reported to have said, "No greater thing could come to our land today than a revival of the spirit of religion. . . . I doubt if there is any problem, social, political or economic, that would not melt away before the fire of such a spiritual awakening."

There are those who would have us believe that the day of mass evangelism is past and who would deny God's own Word, in which He says, "And he gave some evangelists," as though He had discontinued that in this enlightened (?) age. They boast of being up-to-date, when really they are behind the times, for I can show you plenty of evidences that people still want to hear the old story of redeeming grace and never-dying love. There are a lot of poor fellows trying to be erudite and keep up with modern " trends " and stay abreast of the latest theories of some spiritually defunct theological seminary who need to get right with God and preach the Word until heaven opens and the Lord comes down in showers of blessing.

As a preacher and as a Christian and as an American, I

am contributing more to national defense by calling on men to return to God than in any other possible way. For when men get hold of God and God gets hold of men, He can do more for them in five minutes than they can do for themselves in a million years. When God's people get right and sinners are saved, it means better people, better homes, better churches, better communities, better everything. It will turn men from booze to the Bible, women from bridge clubs to prayer meetings. It will enable husbands and wives to live together and find at family altars what divorce courts can never give. It will keep children at home and head off juvenile delinquency. It is the best antidote against suicide, crime, race trouble, business trouble—every kind of trouble. Christians are the salt of the earth and a revival would restore our saltiness, and the more people who are salted, the fewer there are who will spoil, and conditions would be better for their presence. And it would affect this war, for the God who, as Patrick Henry said, " presides over the destinies of nations " and who has interfered in battle ever since He drowned the hosts of Pharaoh and set the stars in their courses against Sisera would come down in power to deliver, if only we could learn that greater than horses and chariots is the help of the Lord our God.

Finally, if you will read verse 7, you will see the reason why we do not have a revival: " There is none that calleth upon thy name, that stirreth up himself to take hold of thee." Mind you, it says, " There is none that STIRRETH UP HIMSELF to take hold of thee." Paul exhorted Timothy, " Stir up the gift of God which is within thee." Here is something God is not going to do for us. He expects us to take ourselves in hand and rouse ourselves, and if ever it was " high time to awake out of sleep " it is now. If you had told me a few years ago that world conditions could come to such a state as we are in today and yet Christians be satisfied to live in such a stupor, I would not have believed it. There is certainly one old hymn that needs to be dusted off and put back into circulation nowadays:

> " Come, Holy Spirit, Heavenly Dove,
>   With all Thy quickening powers,
>   Kindle a flame of sacred love
>   In these cold hearts of ours.
>   In vain we tune our formal songs;
>   In vain we strive to rise;
>   Hosannas languish on our tongues
>   And our devotion dies."

We have heard a lot of the evils of modernism, and certainly we need to stand our ground against " another Gospel." We sometimes shell the woods on the subject of worldliness, and surely there are Demases aplenty who love this present world. But we need to limber up some of our artillery against the sleepiness, the drowsiness, the apathy and lethargy of saints who have been chloroformed by the atmosphere of the age and who, because iniquity abounds, have let their love wax cold. The hardest crowd on earth to reach is found in thousands of church members who know the truth in their heads or who are busy with religious activities all week, but who have never in their lives stirred up themselves to take hold of God. Christians stir themselves to anything but to taking hold of God. Certainly it is not easy. The spirit of the times is against it. Our natural dispositions are against it. The neighbors are against it. Many of our churches are against it. And certainly the devil is against it, for

> " Satan trembles when he sees
>   The weakest saint upon his knees."

But there will never be a revival until God's people are willing to stir up themselves to take hold of God.

Dr. Torrey said:

" I can give a prescription that will bring a revival to any church or community or any city on earth. First, let a few Christians (they need not be many) GET THOROUGHLY RIGHT WITH GOD THEMSELVES. This is the prime essential. If this is not done, the rest I am sorry to say will come to nothing! Second, let them bind themselves together to pray for a revival UNTIL GOD OPENS THE HEAVENS AND COMES DOWN. Third, let them put themselves at the disposal of God to use them as He sees fit in winning others to Christ. That is all. This is sure to bring a revival to any church or community. I have given this prescription around the world. It has been taken by many churches and many communities and in no instance has it ever failed. And it cannot fail."

How can I stir up myself to take hold of God? Get alone with your Bible and take stock of your life, check up, make an inventory, have an honest overhauling in the sight of God. Maybe you will need to take Mr. Finney's suggestion. Get a sheet of paper and write down your sins as God reveals them to you—and never mind how much paper it takes! Make a clean sweep of everything—that pride, that temper, that secret habit, that grumbling, that wicked thing you said about somebody, the way you rob God, your unthankfulness, your neglect of the Bible and all the means of grace. Confess and forsake it all and if you don't feel like praying, pray till you do feel like it. Then claim His gracious promise that if we confess He will forgive, and trust Him by simple faith for the fulness of His Spirit. If you mean business with God He will meet you and bless you as this very chapter declares: " Thou meetest . . . those that remember thee in thy ways."

Mind you, Dr. Torrey said a revival could start with a very few people if they would get thoroughly right with God themselves. I beg of you, do not read this and then lay it down and forget what manner of person you are. Get alone and stir up yourself to take hold of God. If it takes all night, let it take all night, but get back to Bethel and renew the covenant and make a fresh settlement with heaven. Then join yourself with others like-minded to pray for revival until God opens the heavens and comes down. Then go out in full surrender to witness to small and great as God directs you.

Truly, it is time for God to work, for we have made void His law. It is time for God to rend the heavens and come down in old-time showers of blessing. He has done it before and He will do it again, when His people get down to business and stir up themselves to take hold of Him.

VIII

PRESCRIPTION FOR REVIVAL

"If my people, which are called by my name, shall humble them-selves, and pray, and seek my face, and turn from their wicked ways, then will I hear from heaven, and will forgive their sin, and will heal their land."—2 CHRONICLES 7: 14.

THIS is a well-worn verse among revivalists, but there is no danger of exhausting its message today. The need of America is a return to God, and that means, first of all, repentance and revival in the church. What has been said about the weather might be said about revival: everybody talks about it but nobody does anything. There is not much we can do about the weather, but there is plenty we can do about revival.

Thousands of Christians today have no faith for revival. Some believe that because we are in the last days, we need never expect an awakening. But we read that " knowing the time, that now it is high time to awake out of sleep." The fact that we are in the last days was never meant to be a lullaby to put us to sleep but a reveille to wake us up. We can have a revival any time that Christians will pay the price. The fact that Jesus may come at any time should arouse the saints to stir up the gift of God within them. It is just after Paul's description of the coming apostasy that he tells Timothy, " Do the work of an evangelist," and to do real evangelism we must first have revival.

Others think that revivals are a thing of the past, that times have changed, and that such mass movements do not belong today. Instead, we have " revival through educa-tion," building revivals, stewardship revivals. Now, educa-tion and buildings and stewardship have their place in the church, but these things can never compensate for revival. Our great denominational programs today do not give much place to revivals. Of course, there is much good in many of these programs, but it is evident to any honest observer that they are not meeting the situation today. They do some good things, but their approach is not adequate to the need. They simply do not hit the spot. Until the church bodies begin with repentance and humbling before God and confession of sin, these other activities will simply put the cart before the horse. It is true that evangelism is emphasized, but there cannot be effective evangelism until first there is revival. It is after the lost joy of salvation has been restored and we are upheld by God's Spirit that we are able to teach transgressors His ways and that sinners shall be converted unto Him. David had the correct order and it has never changed.

Neither will Bible teaching alone fill the need. There are churches that major in Bible teaching which have not had a revival in years. It is possible to study prophecy, for instance, to the neglect of other great themes, like the work of the Holy Spirit. There is an awful ignorance of that subject these days. It is true that real Bible study should produce revival, just as real revival should produce Bible study, but there is a head-study that does not hide the Word in the heart and the Word does not profit, not being mixed with faith. Hearing but not doing, men deceive themselves.

There are others who are opposed to revivals because to call for revival seems to them a confession of failure and defeat. Some pastors feel that to try to have a revival is an admission of abnormality in the church and that the normal activities of the church should be sufficient. But, regardless of whose fault it is, failure and abnormality mark the church today and it will do no harm but rather good honestly to face the fact, confess it, and do something about it.

Charles G. Finney, who certainly spoke with authority, said:

" Many good men have supposed and still suppose (and I may add, still suppose!) that the best way to promote religion is to go along uniformly and gather in the ungodly gradually and without excitement. But however sound such reasoning may appear in the abstract, the facts demonstrate its futility."

Others have been turned against revivals by the extremism and extravagances of some traveling preachers. Of course, this is foolish, for we could abandon every phase of Christian work if we thus looked at the evils of some workers. Some have concluded that the pastor can do all the work of the ministry and would rule out God's order of " prophets, evangelists, teachers." There is a special work for the revivalist and evangelist. Once again, Mr. Finney said:

" There is a point on which most ministers fail. They know not how to wake up the church and raise the tone of piety to a high standard and thus clear the way for a work of conversion. THERE IS ONLY HERE AND THERE A MINISTER IN THE COUNTRY WHO KNOWS HOW TO PROBE THE CHURCH WHEN IT IS IN A COLD AND BACKSLIDDEN CONDITION SO AS TO EFFECTUALLY WAKEN THE MEMBERS AND KEEP THEM AWAKE. The members of the church sin against such light that when they become cold it is very hard to rouse them. They have a form of piety which wards off the truth, while at the same time it is just that kind of piety that has no power or efficiency. They are often employed about the machinery of religion and pass for good Christians, but they are of no use in a revival."

There are others who realize that we need revival, but they substitute a false and carnal stir, whipped up by mere human excitement for the genuine work of the Spirit of God. We live in an age that must be amused and entertained, and some have put on glorified shows and religious circuses that attract crowds and temporarily excite the people, but the last state of most of them is worse than the first. It is better to have no revival than to have a counterfeit. The serious and solemn searching of souls by the preaching of the Word is too holy a thing for any man to dare to imitate.

But, no matter how many do not believe in revival nor how many arguments may be brought to bear against it, there is absolutely no way for the church today to regain her power in a world gone mad except through the way of our text, humility, repentance and a return to God. Americans need to read the history of our nation and learn that whatever we have today worth talking about we owe to Christianity and that the Christian fires in America have been kept burning through old-fashioned revivals. To hear some Americans talk, you would never think religion had anything to do with our progress. Too many college students know about explorers and generals and politicians, but know little about the revivalists in our national life. Jonathan Edwards and Whitefield and Wesley and Asbury and Roger Williams and Timothy Dwight and Finney and Cartwright and a host of others of their kind meant more to America than all the politicians.

But, dark as this hour may be, there is every reason to believe we can and may have revival. In the same year that Butler published his *Analogy,* saying that " amongst all people of discernment, it was taken for granted that Christianity was fictitious,"—in that very year John Wesley was converted! God had other arrangements! But if we have revival, we shall have to do more than merely start another movement. We are great people at starting movements, but we won't move! We will join the "National Association for Proclamation of Revival," but we won't revive!

The way to revival is outlined in our text. "IF MY PEOPLE, WHICH ARE CALLED BY MY NAME . . ." The application today is to us Christians who bear the name of Christ. A revival is God's people getting right with God. And whether there is a revival or not depends on what they do. It hangs on an "IF." Revivals do not just "happen," like a thunderstorm some afternoon. This idea that if we pray and pray, maybe sometime something will crash down on us and make us all be better and feel better is not true. If we meet certain conditions we have a revival, just as when farmers meet certain conditions they raise a crop. It is indeed a work of God, but it turns on what we do: the Word does not say "IF GOD . . ." but "IF MY PEOPLE . . . SHALL HUMBLE THEMSELVES." We ask God to make us humble, but God asks us to humble ourselves. "Whosoever therefore shall humble himself as this little child, the same is greatest in the kingdom of heaven" (Matt. 18: 4). "He that shall humble himself shall be exalted" (Matt. 23: 12). "Humble yourselves in the sight of the Lord and he shall lift you up" (Jas. 4: 10). "Humble yourselves therefore under the mighty hand of God, that he may exalt you in due time" (1 Pet. 5: 6). To humble ourselves is not merely to have pious feelings, but to acknowledge our lowly estate before God, confess our sins against Him and be willing to eat humble pie before our fellow men in confessing our faults one to another, making restitution for wrong we have done and esteeming others better than ourselves in all lowliness of mind. This is about the last thing most Christians are willing to do, so there are few revivals. We try to have a revival and save our faces, but the first thing we must lose is our face!

"AND PRAY." Everybody agrees that prayer is a fine thing, but nobody does much praying. Prayer that brings revival is hard work. The flesh resents it, our minds quickly cloud up, our tongues cleave to the roof of the mouth, we think of everything else and we quickly excuse ourselves. If our Lord taught anything, He taught importunate prayer, as in the parables of the woman and the judge and the man calling at midnight for bread. And Jesus practised it, for He prayed all night more than once. If He who always lived in the Father's will needed to pray all night, what shall we needy creatures say about ourselves?

" AND SEEK MY FACE." To seek God's face is to seek God's approval, His smile, the light of His countenance upon us. Does the favor of God rest on your life? Are you in communion with Him? We need to renew the covenant, to go back to Bethel and dwell there. We have sought everything else in our churches, we have courted the favor of the world, and in seeking it we have lost what favor we did have, we have lost the world's respect. If we had spent our time getting on better terms with God, we should have had power both with God and men. We have had preachers who have sought to please the Athenians, ever chasing a new thing, who have learned to review books and dabble a little in literature and philosophy, but they are making no dent on this generation. Yet God raised up unlettered Dwight L. Moody and shook nations with him because Moody sought the face of God, not the favor of men. When Paul was called to preach, he conferred not with flesh and blood. He went to Arabia and got better acquainted with God. We have enough big preachers and important churches: we need preachers and churches who know the secret of the Lord, with the stamp of Divine approval on them.

" AND TURN FROM THEIR WICKED WAYS." This part of God's prescription is definitely out of style today. Preachers who dare to speak of the sins of the saints are considered unethical, negative fault-finders. Days of prayer have been proclaimed, but if we go to church to hear the minister read or pray a formal petition to God, then go out lugging our sins along, we might as well have stayed at home. Politely admitting that we have all done wrong is very fashionable these days, but there is no repentance in it. There must be a definite, deliberate breaking with our sins. "Whoso confesseth AND FORSAKETH his sins shall have mercy."

Sin is simply having our own way. "We have turned every one to his own way." Real repentance is not merely turning from this particular sin and that, but turning from having our way and letting God have His way.

"THEN WILL I HEAR FROM HEAVEN, AND WILL FORGIVE THEIR SIN, AND WILL HEAL THEIR LAND." You see, when we do certain things, then God does certain things. "IF MY PEOPLE . . . THEN WILL I . . ." And there is blessing not only for the individual but for the land. Isaiah confessed individual guilt, "I am a man of unclean lips," and then national guilt, "I dwell in the midst of a people of unclean lips." Here God promises to hear and forgive the individual and then to heal the land. When American Christians and churches turn to God, it will mean blessing on all America. A revival in the church always brings blessings that overflow the church.

Here then is God's prescription. But it is cleverly drowned out today with drives and campaigns and programs and religious retreats and spiritual emphasis weeks. It is unpopular, for nobody likes to humble himself and pray and seek God's face and turn from his wicked ways. It is much more pleasant to put on a picnic or get up a play or prepare a stunt for the next meeting. So the dead keep on burying the dead. But God's prescription knows no substitute for all our concoctions that claim to be "just as good."

IX

FOOLS, FACTS AND FIRE

"Fools for Christ's sake."—1 CORINTHIANS 4: 10.
"Preach the Word."—2 TIMOTHY 4: 2.
"Stir up the gift of God.—2 TIMOTHY 1: 6.

OVER thirty years ago, in the foothills of the Blue Ridge Mountains, alone in the woods on a summer afternoon, I came to Christ and believed His promise, "Him that cometh unto me I will in no wise cast out." I had been brought up in a Christian home, under old-fashioned preaching—sin black, hell hot, judgment certain, eternity long, and salvation free. I was converted during an old-fashioned revival—not a modern, fashionable, harmless little revival, but an old-fashioned revival that stirred the saints and saved sinners and set the angels rejoicing and put the devil's program in reverse. I mean an old-fashioned "Amazing Grace," "How Firm a Foundation," "Blest Be the Tie That Binds" sort of revival, where "grace taught our hearts to fear and grace our fears relieved; how precious did that grace appear the hour we first believed!" They didn't "hold" revivals in those days, they turned them loose!

I do not remember that any particular sermon brought me under conviction. I knew that I was lost, that Christ died for me, and that the gift of God was eternal life. My father and mother taught me that and prepared me for that summer afternoon when I simply took God at His Word and, after all,

"What more can He say than to us He hath said,
To us who for refuge to Jesus have fled?"

I remember that I came back home through the woods to my father's little shop, and I didn't go in through the door —I went through the window and we embraced each other in the joy of my new experience. That was back in the days before the devil had a monopoly on enthusiasm. That was before these strange times came along, when sinners can weep in theaters over the glycerin tears of Hollywood divorcées, while the saints are ashamed to weep in church over a lost and dying world.

That afternoon I went out at supper time to do the chores, and I went singing:

> " Jesus, I my cross have taken,
> All to leave and follow Thee;
> Destitute, despised, forsaken,
> Thou from hence my all shalt be."

If I didn't have much theology in my head, I had a lot of doxology in my heart! I have often thought since that I could take half a dozen of those old-fashioned, red-hot Christians of those days, who knew but two or three things but knew them through and through and up and down and in and out—that I could take a few of those old Christians and go places for God while a lot of modern church members are discussing ways and means, pouring hot chocolate, and reading the minutes of the last meeting!

Since my conversion, I have had the usual ups and downs of a Christian and a preacher trying to get located in the jig-saw puzzle of the present-day confusion of the saints. I have mixed and mingled with all shades and grades and varieties and degrees, from the Big Shots—some of whom turn out to be just buckshot when you get to know them!— down to some who have never learned that it takes more than a three-cornered hat to make a Napoleon out of a corporal! I have worked in different kinds of churches.

I have labored with those Sunday-morning saints whose religion consists of a little Ladies' Aid, lemonade, and a little money in a duplex envelope. For a while I was among the modernists. At one time I thought I didn't know enough to be a modernist, but eventually I discovered that you don't have to know much!

Finally, by the grace of God, I landed among the fundamentalists. "Landed" may not be the right word, for a lot of them are still at sea! I have never been able to understand why they call us fundamentalists a dull and colorless crowd. I think we are the most interesting collection of human specimens that ever came along. There are, for instance, the professional come-outers, religious gypsies, church grasshoppers who never can find a church or preacher good enough for them. They remind us of the old brother who used to sing above everybody else and completely out of tune:

> "Sweet prospects, sweet birds and sweet flowers
> Have all lost their fragrance BUT ME!"

It was one of this sort who had already belonged to three denominations and was getting ready to join a fourth. He announced his intention to his pastor *pro tem,* for any pastor he had was *pro tem!* The old pastor, wise to the ways of all such, replied, "Well, I don't think it does any harm to change labels on an empty bottle!"

Then we have the porcupine Christians—they have a lot of good points but you can't get near them!

And by the time you have listened to one crowd explain the two natures and another the three natures; one crowd explain why the church will go through the great tribulation and another explain why it will not; one crowd explain why the Roman Empire will be revived and another explain why it will not; one crowd explain why we may have a revival

and another why we will not—by the time you have listened
to all that, you will readily agree that while we may lack
a lot of things in the camp of the fundamentalists, variety is
not one of them!

But " with all their faults, I love them still " (of course,
most of them are not very still), because I feel that most
of them have the root of the matter in them. Sometimes
they grow pretty stubborn, like the Scotsman who said he
was open to conviction but would like to see the man who
could convince him! And some of them do funny things,
like getting out on a limb with Mussolini (I don't think
Mussolini has caused the Italian nation half the embarrass-
ment he has caused some Bible teachers!). But for a' that,
I love them still, for they believe in the Book, the Blood
and the Blessed Hope, and I expect to see them all get together in heaven, even if they can't do it down here.

But sometimes I do wish that these dividers of the Word,
who take it apart much better than they ever get it back
together, would agree a little better. Just when I am
stretched out and resting on some good verse, some expositor
shows up like a policeman to order me off private property
and tell me that this verse is reserved for the Jew and that
for the Kingdom Age. I have heard of a man without a
country and I had almost decided once that these Word-
Dividers were going to leave me a preacher without a Bible,
and I began to wonder, " Is this the communion of saints
or the confusion of tongues? " Finally, I took refuge in
the text: " Let God be true, but every man a liar."

Sometimes I have thought that I'd like to go back again
to the old days at Corinth Baptist Church, where I grew up,
where we used to enjoy the spiritual food without arguing
too much about the recipe. I have noticed that folks who
are most finicky about their food usually have dyspepsia.
Two things make a good meal, good food and a good ap-

petite. And the best preparation for the Bread of Life is a good, hearty appetite.

Josh Billings is reported to have said, " I'd rather know a few things for certain than be sure of a lot of things that ain't so." There are a few things I believe for certain, and I leave you to quibble over the details. For one thing, I am certain that the Bible is the Word of God. Either it is or it isn't, and either all of it is the Word of God or we never can be sure of any of it. It is either absolute or obsolete. If we have to start changing this verse, toning down that, apologizing for this and making allowances for that, we might as well give up, so we must take it as it is or leave it alone.

I believe, furthermore, that " all have sinned," that man is lost and in need of a Saviour. I must confess that I am not much impressed with the human race. The heart is deceitful and desperately wicked and man is no better than he ever was. His head and hands have outrun his heart, and if you scratch off the varnish of civilization, you discover the same old savage, who has merely discovered more terrible ways of being low-down and horrible. For further information read your newspaper! I never say that civilization is going to the dogs. I still have some respect for dogs. Mankind without the grace of God is doing things beneath the dignity of the beasts of the field. I read a story of a hog that got drunk, and when the other hogs would have nothing to do with him, he said, " If you'll excuse me for acting like a man, I never will do it again! "

But I also believe that " God so loved the world that he gave his only begotten Son." I have read books and heard sermons on the atonement and most of them have confused more than they have clarified. It is always easier to understand what the Bible says than to understand what somebody thinks it meant to say. Barabbas should have had a clear understanding of the atonement, for he could have said literally, " He put himself in my place," and that is what Christ did for us all.

> " Upon a life I did not live;
> Upon a death I did not die,
> Another's life, Another's death,
> I stake my whole eternity."

And then I am so glad that " whosoever believeth on him shall not perish but have everlasting life." I am so glad that it is not " whosoever feeleth a certain way, whosoever seeth a vision or dreameth a dream or prayeth through." What a time I used to have trying to understand what the brethren meant by " saving faith " ! I grew up in the county next to A. C. Dixon's home county in North Carolina, and have preached in churches his father used to serve. I have thought often of how as a boy he read *Pilgrim's Progress* and was brought into a miserable frame of mind. He cried because he couldn't cry, was burdened because he wasn't burdened, distressed because he wasn't distressed. Finally, he went to church, and after his father had preached on how to be saved, Clarence went to the mourner's bench, and when his father came along and asked how it was with him, he replied that he was trusting Jesus and his father made it plain that that was all he was expected to do. How many grow confused right there and try to have faith in their faith instead of faith in the Lord!

These are a " few things for certain " which I believe with all my heart. There is much that I don't understand; if I could understand it, there wouldn't be much in it! I don't understand predestination but I believe that I am chosen in Him. I don't understand all about the security of the saints but I believe that I am a child of God and that, while my Father may discipline me, He will never disown me. I am not an expert in prophecy but I am not looking for the kingdom without the King. I know that some make a glorified hobby of prophecy, being occupied with His coming but not occupying till He come. I know that some are always studying the meaning of the fourth toe of the right foot of some beast in prophecy and have never used either foot to go and bring men to Christ. I do not know who the 666 is in Revelation but I know this world is sick, sick, sick, and the best way to speed the Lord's return is to win more souls for Him. I could lecture on " The Rise and Fall of Hitler's Mustache " and get a crowd, but if I spoke on " Obedience " you couldn't get some saints out to church with a rope and tackle. They don't believe in amusements but they want to be amused!

Now, if you ask me, " What is the supreme need of the hour? " I would say, in the light of our texts, that we need FOOLS for Christ's sake with the FACTS of the Word set on FIRE from Above.

There is something lacking among Bible Christians today. If you are aware of it, I need not describe it; if you are not aware of it, you would not understand if I did describe it. I have no fancy name for it. You may call it " the filling of the Spirit," " full surrender," " consecration," " the victorious life," " revival." Unfortunately, too many of us have argued over the expressions without having the experience. Whatever it is, most of us haven't it! Let us put it this way, that we need a new experience of the Lord in the hearts of His people.

Too much of our orthodoxy is correct and sound but, like words without a tune, statutes without songs, it does not glow and burn, it does not stir the wells of the heart, it has lost its hallelujah, it is too much like a catechism and not enough like a camp meeting. You may smile at our spiritual forbears, call them primitive and antiquated; but they had a vividness and a vitality, a fervor and a fire, that make us look like fireflies beside their flaming torches. One man with a glowing experience of God is worth a library full of arguments.

We need a heart warming. It is one thing to commemorate Aldersgate and talk about what God did to John Wesley; it is another thing to have our own hearts strangely warmed. The early Christians did not need a shot in the arm every Sunday to keep them going. They knew Jesus and they upset the world and worried the devil and gave wicked rulers insomnia and started something that jails couldn't lock up, fire couldn't burn, water couldn't drown, swords couldn't kill. The church needs dare-saints instead of more diplomats. This world has never been moved by cold, calculating brass hats but by FOOLS, with their FACTS on FIRE.

You may belittle experience and speak of the dangers of emotion, but we are suffering today from a species of Christianity as dry as dust, as cold as ice, as pale as a corpse, and as dead as King Tut. We are suffering, not from a lack of correct heads but of consumed hearts. Alexander Maclaren said:

" There is a type of intellectual preacher who is always preaching down enthusiasm and preaching up what they call sober standards of feeling in matters of religion, by which in nine cases out of ten they mean exactly such a tepid condition as is described in much less polite language when the voice of heaven says, ' Because thou art neither cold nor hot but lukewarm, I will spew thee out of my mouth.' It was not Erasmus, the polished, learned, scintillating, mighty intellect of his time, who made Germany over; it was rough, rugged Martin Luther with a conviction and compassion as deep as life."

God forgive us, in an hour like this, that we have been dry Christians, preaching a dynamite Gospel and living firecracker lives. Let us get alone with God, confess our sins, claim the cleansing blood, be filled with the Spirit, and go out to be Christ's FOOLS, with our FACTS on FIRE!

[77]

X

"BUT WE SEE JESUS"

"But now we see not yet all things put under him. But we see Jesus. . . ."—HEBREWS 2: 8, 9.

OVER the entrance to the Union Station in our national capital there is written this inscription:

" Fire, greatest of discoveries, enabling man to live in various climates, use many foods and compel the forces of nature to do his work. Electricity, carrier of light and power, devourer of time and space, greatest servant of man, yet itself unknown."

And then there follows this quotation from the Bible, " Thou hast put all things under his feet."

Now, whoever was responsible for that inscription must not have understood his text thoroughly, for it does not refer to man, in the last analysis, but to Christ, the Son of Man. God indeed made the first Adam to have dominion over the earth, but he lost it; and the only way he ever will regain it will be through the last Adam, Jesus Christ. Adam was conquered by sin but Christ conquered the devil. Adam was conquered by death but Christ overcame death. Adam lost the tree of life but Christ regained it, and " blessed are they that do his commandments that they may have a right " to it. Adam lost Paradise but Christ made possible a new Paradise by the River of Life. Adam lost his dominion, he never has regained it and never will. He is still trying to regain it with fire and electricity and all the wit and wisdom of unregenerate human nature, but never was it more evident than now that " WE SEE NOT YET ALL THINGS PUT UNDER MAN."

I know that he flies the air, talks on the wind, has dug deeply into the treasures of knowledge. But instead of putting all things under his feet, he himself is buried under a landslide of his own devices. He is being eaten by the Frankenstein which he himself created. A leading university professor admitted some time ago, " The world we have created is too much for us. The wisdom of the race has failed before the problems which the race has raised." We were promised Paradise but we have pandemonium. The trail from protoplasm to perfection has run out in the wilderness. During the Century of Progress exhibition of some years ago, someone wrote:

" The theme was the achievements of science and their application through industry to the creation of a larger life for all mankind. The achievements of science were in abundance but where, one was moved to ask, was the evidence of a larger life for mankind or even the promise of it? "

I know that we have come from tallow candles to television, but there is also more suffering, sin, suicide, insanity, crime, immorality, infidelity, than the world has ever known. And so far as progress is concerned, one thinks of the family discussing an absent relative when someone remarked, " He's getting on in the world," and grandmother from her rocking chair in the corner asked, " Which world? " We live in a fairyland of wonders devised by the head and fashioned by the hand; but while man has been going places with head and hand, his heart has been left behind. What a joke, then, to crown him with the laurels of victory when he staggers with moral drunkenness and spiritual delirium tremens. No, " WE SEE NOT YET ALL THINGS PUT UNDER MAN."

Indeed, we may go a step farther and say, " WE SEE NOT YET ALL THINGS PUT UNDER THE CHRIS-

TIAN." I know that Christ overcame the world and we stand in His victory. I know that " greater is he that is in us than he that is in the world," and that " this is the victory that overcometh the world, even our faith." But all things are not yet ACTUALLY under the Christian. We are " troubled on every side, yet not distressed; perplexed, but not in despair; persecuted, but not forsaken; cast down, but not destroyed." In this world we have tribulation. We share the common ups and downs of humanity, its sunshine and shadow, its weal and woe. Sometimes our bank account is down and our blood pressure is up. We are going to heaven but we have not yet arrived. WE SEE NOT YET ALL THINGS PUT UNDER THE CHRISTIAN.

Furthermore, WE SEE NOT YET ALL THINGS PUT UNDER CHRIST. True, God has put all things under His feet but WE SEE not yet all things put under Him. True, at Calvary and the open grave He triumphed once for all. But we see not yet the actual and final consummation of His triumph; it is a mystery and not yet a full manifestation. The devil still goes around as a roaring lion and, worse still, as an angel of light. Sin still blights the race and death still reaps its grim harvest. We live in perilous times and the world lies in wickedness. WE SEE NOT YET ALL THINGS PUT UNDER CHRIST. But there are two words for " see" in this passage. One means the impression our eyes receive and the other means " intently to behold." As we look around, the impression that our eyes receive is, WE SEE NOT YET ALL THINGS PUT UNDER MAN, OR PUT UNDER THE CHRISTIAN, OR PUT UNDER CHRIST. But we intently behold JESUS, and I know nothing better than to assist you in off-looking unto Jesus, the Author and Finisher of our faith.

Certainly, there is much today that " we see not yet put

under him " or put under us. There are those who, if I
should ask, " Have all your sorrows and your fears, your
troubles and your tears, been put under you? " would have
to answer, " No, brother, would to God they were, but I
see not yet all these put under me." There are old heartaches and new ones. There are those who lately have
rained tears over an open grave. There are those whose
castles have tumbled, whose dreams have faded, who are
sad because there is such a distance between what they are
and what they had hoped to be. But if you see not yet
all your troubles put away, see Jesus! Fix your eyes on
the " Man of sorrows and acquainted with grief," who said,
" Let not your heart be troubled," and who has guaranteed
us that if we only trust Him, at a time not too far distant,
God shall wipe all tears from our eyes.

I think when some saints die the devil will say, " Well, I
don't care if he does go to heaven. I've had a lot of fun
worrying him down here. One day he thought he was
saved and the next day he didn't know. I've worried him all
his life." Brother, you can sit on the north side of religion
with your teeth rattling if you like, but I don't intend to
give the devil that much pleasure. I believe in living in
the SON-shine of the Presence of the Lord by looking unto
Jesus.

There are others who are fully aware that sickness and
death have not yet been finally put under Him. Jesus was
and is the Great Physician, but we still await the redemption of the body. And some have learned in more ways
than one what it means to " groan in this tabernacle."
Salvation is free, but it is not yet full in our actual experience: if it were, some of you wouldn't be wearing glasses
and trying to chew with false teeth! Maybe the doctor has
shaken his head and told you that you can never be your
old self again. Well, if Christ is our life, though we may
never be our old selves again, soon we shall be like Him,

for when He shall appear we shall be like Him! So, as Christians, we can " feel better when we feel bad than we used to feel when we felt good! "

Then, we are all conscious, I am sure, that we see not yet sin and Satan actually put under us. The devil is on his way to the bottomless pit and the lake of fire, but he has not yet arrived. And how grieved we often are over the deceitfulness of our own hearts, for " those who fain would serve Him best are conscious most of wrong within."

But if we are disappointed in ourselves, we have a High Priest who was tempted in all points as we are, yet without sin. John Bunyan relates:

" Again one day as I was passing in the field and that too with some dashes in my conscience, suddenly the sentence fell upon my soul, ' Thy righteousness is in heaven.' And methought withal I saw with the eyes of my soul Jesus Christ at God's right hand. I saw also, moreover, that it was not my good frame of heart that made my righteousness better, nor my bad frame of heart that made my righteousness worse, for my righteousness was Jesus Christ Himself, the same yesterday, today and forever."

In other words, John Bunyan saw not yet all sin removed from John Bunyan, but he saw Jesus!

But perhaps you have grown cynical. Looking at other Christians, looking at some Bible teacher or conference or school or church, you have grown disillusioned and have said, " Alas, I see not yet all things put under Him there." Well, perhaps it will teach you to see Jesus instead of men and to remember that " then were the disciples glad when they saw the Lord." You went to a much advertised place to hear a much advertised preacher, but your idol's feet were of clay and very poor clay at that, and now you are sick at heart. I have never yet seen a church or school where I thought all things had been put under Christ, but I can see Jesus! When the disciples failed to cast out the demon from the boy at the foot of the mount of transfiguration, Jesus said, " Bring him to me." We hear a lot about the failures of the church today, and too often has it been true of churches before a demonized world that " they could not." But back of the church stands Christ and He never fails; His touch still has its ancient power. I know that we live in the Laodicean age of a lukewarm church, but even that chapter does not end there but with Christ Himself knocking at the door of human hearts. Let us see Jesus! We see not yet all things put under Him in the church, but we see Him! I know that there is envy and strife and discord aplenty, that fundamentalism needs a trip to the mourner's bench more than anything else. I sympathize with the little girl who prayed, " Lord, make all the bad people good and make all the good people nice." Yes, there is grace without graces, as there are graces without grace. But above all the failures of Christians and churches we see Jesus!

Finally, as we look out on a wretched, miserable world, with the newspapers flaming screamlines and our young generation looking down a gun barrel for its future, truly " we see not yet all things put under him." But there is a crumb of comfort even in all this: in the breakdown of this Punch-and-Judy civilization, some are beginning to discover that the faith of our fathers is not the back-number proposition some sophomore smart alecks thought it was. And some who regarded prophetic teachers as crape-hangers with " bats in our belfries " may learn that we are not the ones who " missed the bus." Of course, we do not want to pat ourselves on the back with an " I-told-you-so " attitude in these days. Yet I am reminded of a half-wit in a certain town who did not have much sense, but he had enough to get saved, which is more than a lot of people are using these days. The townspeople put up with his witnessing because they regarded him as a harmless nitwit. But an earthquake struck the town, split it open, tumbled buildings and brought men to their knees in prayer for the first time in their lives. That morning this converted half-wit came down town and it was his big morning. Every time he found one of these merchants on his knees he would strike him on the back and shout, " Now who's right? Thank God, my ticket's bought and baggage checked; come on, Jesus, I'm ready to go! " It is a great thing to have your ticket bought and baggage checked today!

Yes, we see not yet all things put under Him, but we see Jesus. One thing cheers my heart amid the tears and fears, the war of words and strife of tongues today, the darkness and despair of a crumbling world—thank God, I'm on the winning side! In Acts we read that King Herod made a big speech one day and the people said, " It is the voice of a god and not of a man." Then we read, " And immediately the angel of the Lord smote him because he gave not God the glory: and he was eaten of worms and gave up the ghost." Then notice the contrast of the next verse: " But the word of God grew and prevailed." It has always been like that: you are for the WORD or you are for the WORMS, not only worms that get the body but the worm that dieth not, where the fire is not quenched.

More than one Herod has risen through the ages to shake his fist at God, but the worms got them all. What if Nero did wear a crown worth half a million, go fishing with golden fishhooks, never wear the same clothes twice—the worms got him just the same! But the Word grows on and prevails. An earlier Herod tried to kill Jesus, but, later, God said to Joseph in Egypt, " You can take the child back now. FOR THEY ARE DEAD WHICH SOUGHT THE YOUNG CHILD'S LIFE." They always die when they get in the way of God's business.

From the way some Christians talk, you would think this war took God by surprise. But never worry, God is still on the throne. Let the kings of the earth set themselves and the rulers take counsel against God and His Christ, but He that sits in the heavens shall laugh and the Lord shall have them in derision. It may look like the devil has it going his way, but when the smoke has cleared, you will discover that God is putting His program through according to schedule.

Some time ago, I left Baltimore on a Sunday night to make a speaking appointment in Illinois by Monday night. I was due to arrive there just thirty minutes before speaking time and, with railroad schedules like they are now, it looked hopeless. But I felt that I was going to do it. Next morning I discovered that a prominent government official was sitting across the aisle from me in the Pullman. He had to speak that night in Chicago, and I understand that orders were given the engineer that the train must go through on time. But I got a lot of fun out of that situation. I said to myself afterwards, " That big official thought the train was making time because he had to speak in Chicago, but the Lord was really overruling it all so this preacher could preach on time that same night! " Oh, brother, it sometimes appears that this world is running the show, but back of all the plans of men God is making all things work together for good for His own! God had the first word and He'll have the last, and though we see not yet all things put under Him, we see Jesus, who said, " Fear not, I am the first and the last."

So, as you go out into this puzzled and distracted world, see Jesus. Above your sorrows and your tears, see Jesus. Above your aches and pains, see Jesus. Above the failures in yourself and others, see Jesus. Above the world's sin and shame, see Jesus. Let not the things you see not yet keep you from seeing Jesus. Let not self nor Satan, saint nor sinner, divert your eye from Him. Change and decay in all around you see, but He abideth faithful. He remaineth, the same yesterday, the historic Christ; the same today, the indwelling Christ; the same tomorrow, the coming Christ. He is behind us, within us, ahead of us. We don't know what's ahead, but we know Who's ahead. He was born on time, died on time, rose on time, is coming on time. He may seem slow, but He is never late. He is the First and the Last, so there is nothing to fear; He was here before there ever was anything to fear, and He'll be here after all we fear has passed away.

Did you ever sit in a train in a railroad station, looking out a window, and feel that it was moving, when, actually, it was another train that was moving and yours was still standing? This world is a passing show: " The world passeth away and the lust thereof," " The fashion of this world passeth away," and sometimes we are carried along by the urge and surge of it. We need to look out the other window and fix our eyes upon Jesus, looking full into His wonderful face. Then indeed the things of this world will grow strangely dim in the light of His glory and grace. " We see not yet all things put under Him. BUT WE SEE JESUS."

XI

CHRIST, THE GREAT DIVIDER

"Think not that I am come to send peace on earth: I came not to send peace, but a sword. For I am come to set a man at variance against his father, and the daughter against her mother, and the daughter-in-law against her mother-in-law. And a man's foes shall be they of his own household. He that loveth father or mother more than me is not worthy of me: and he that loveth son or daughter more than me is not worthy of me. And he that taketh not his cross, and followeth after me, is not worthy of me. He that findeth his life shall lose it: and he that loseth his life for my sake shall find it."
—MATTHEW 10: 34–39.

THERE is a lot of sentimental preaching to the effect that Jesus is the Great Unifier of the human race and that the principles of Jesus will eventually weld this world into one great brotherhood of sweetness and light. But every newspaper tells us that something has gone wrong with these fair-weather prophets. Jesus does unify those who are in Him. He is the head of the church and in Him believers may have one accord, the unity of the Spirit. It doesn't always appear that way, considering how the saints differ and split and subdivide. Nevertheless, they should and can have unity of spirit in the Lord.

But there is all the difference in the universe between the relation of Christ to His own and to the world at large. Jesus Christ is the most divisive force in existence. He has caused more division than all other forces since creation. He has divided more hearts, more homes, more churches, more communities, more nations, than all other forces put together. Away with this modern, oily, smooth talk about Jesus! One of the tragedies of our times is that too many people are saying nice things about Jesus and then doing nothing about it. They are patting Him on the back, writing poems about Him, drawing pictures of Him, putting Him in church windows, but while they draw nigh Him with their mouths and honor Him with their lips, their hearts are far from Him. Professing to know God, in works they deny Him and are abominable and disobedient and unto every good work reprobate. They call Him Lord, Lord, and do not what He says.

Away with such hypocrisy about Jesus! He never stood for that when He was here. He declared, " He that is not with me is against me; and he that gathereth not with me scattereth abroad." He could endure people spitting in His face and crucifying Him better than two-faced individuals, neither " fish nor fowl." He prayed for soldiers driving spikes through His quivering flesh, " Father, forgive them, for they know not what they do "; but of these half-and-half, tasteless souls like salt without savor He said, " Because thou art neither cold nor hot, I will spew thee out of my mouth."

God would rather a man be on the wrong side of the fence than to try to sit on it. I am reminded of the man out in Kansas who, during a revival, was asked whether he wanted to go to heaven. He replied, " No." Then he was asked, " Do you want to go to hell? " and he answered, " No." Finally, when asked, " Where do you want to go? " he replied, " I'd just as soon live right on in Kansas! " It is fashionable these days to say nice things about Jesus without personal committal. But Jesus is not looking for compliments, He is looking for confession, for people who mean business with Him.

Men's hearts are revealed by the attitude they take toward Jesus. Simeon said of the baby Jesus in the temple, " This child is set for the fall and rising again of many in Israel; and for a sign which shall be spoken against . . . THAT THE THOUGHTS OF MANY HEARTS MAY BE REVEALED " (Lk. 2: 34, 35). You cannot tell who is who in town by the house in which they live, for some saints may live on back streets and some of the crooks on Main. You cannot tell by education, social position, church standing. But there is one test that never fails: Jesus Christ stands in the middle of town with His dividing sword, and splits the town in two, and in the last analysis there are just two kinds of people there. We divide them into rich and poor, black and white, educated and illiterate—all grades, from the down-and-outs to the up-and-outs. But it is not the Blue Book of society or the bank book of finance or the church book of religion that really shows where we belong: it is God's Book that classifies us, and at the last day it won't matter whether we drove a Pierce-Arrow or pushed an apple cart through town. What will matter will be, What did we do about Jesus?

Some years ago, when King George V of England was being buried, we listened to the broadcast and heard that old hymn used often at the funeral of the commonest day laborer:

> " Swift to its close ebbs out life's little day;
> Earth's joys grow dim, its glories pass away;
> Change and decay in all around I see;
> O Thou who changest not, abide with me."

And after all, whether it be the king or cobbler, the only thing that matters at the funeral is, On which side of the Great Divider did he stand?

So Christ stands among us today and splits asunder the human race, to the right and to the left. And as I look over congregations, I try to visualize the Unseen Divider who came not to bring peace but a sword. Often the audience looks united enough, but I try to remember, " There is an unseen line that separates us tonight as far apart as East from West, as heaven from hell. ' He that believeth on him is not condemned: but he that believeth not is condemned already '—there the line runs! " And I have often wondered what would happen if, in the midst of my sermon, He would appear and begin to show us just where that line runs throughout the congregation. What a zigzag line it would be! Over here husband and wife might be separated, for although they touch each other here tonight, they may be as far apart as all eternity. Over there it may be father and son; over yonder the line may run between mother and daughter. What would the crowd look like when He got through? Some people might not look so indifferent and bored, some might wake up if they really saw themselves divided to the right and left. And yet that line is here, whether we see it or not, for we are on one side of Jesus or the other.

Jesus is either a sanctuary or a snare (Isa. 8: 14), and either we become more drawn to Him or more hardened against Him. The sun shines on clay and hardens it, and the sun shines on ice and melts it: so do human hearts respond to Christ as presented in the Gospel. Just as a blacksmith's hands grow calloused and a barefoot boy's feet grow tough, so do hearts harden against truth rejected. A child may step on fresh cement and leave an impression; but when it hardens, an elephant may tread upon it and leave no mark. Is your heart hardening toward Jesus?

A man relates that once he was caught in a boat far from shore during a storm and that for one hour he faced what seemed certain death:

" It was strange [he said] how everything in my life changed value out there facing death. It was like looking through the other end of a telescope. Things unimportant suddenly loomed large and things I had deemed of first concern shriveled away. That poker game I had boasted about looked very small; but there came to mind that old

Negro mammy who had helped bring me up, and I remembered some of the hymns she sang. Everything shifted in a hurry out there facing death."

Yes, in an hour like that the important thing is where we stand with the Great Divider.

You may fool your wife and children, the church and pastor; you may be thought a person of character and influence, but in the white light of His Presence all sham and camouflage are stripped away. We quickly come down to our right size in His sight. When our Lord was on earth He deflated a lot of human balloons. He was all love and tenderness when some soul in need came to Him honestly and humbly; but when pompous Pharisees showed up, He took the wind out of their sails in short order. And in this day, when we are hearing that " all men are good at heart," when false prophets are preaching peace when there is no peace, we need to hear our Lord say afresh, " I came not to bring peace but a sword."

Jesus divides the individual. The moment He enters the heart, a new nature is implanted there, and the Christian discovers a conflict between the old man and the new. He finds himself in the seventh chapter of Romans, and if he lets the Spirit have control, he will move out into the glorious victory of the eighth chapter, but all his life he will remember that he has both the Spirit and the flesh. Oh, I know that some people say they never have conflict, and I am uneasy about them. Maybe they never run into the devil because they are going the same direction he is traveling! You have to head the other way to meet the devil. The best saints of God through the ages realized that when the Great Divider enters the life, He divides the old from the new, and they did not bask in a rocking-chair under a shade tree; they wrestled with God, and watched and prayed, and they were under no illusions as to the fight of faith. For, no matter how you explain the fight of faith, it is still a fight, and we wrestle with powerful adversaries. Dr. Torrey pointed out that those who think they have reached some sublime height of faith and trust because they never know any agony of conflict or prayer have certainly gotten beyond their Lord and all the heroes of faith. The Great Divider brings division and there is victory only in Him.

Jesus divides families. He stated that plainly in our text. Everywhere I go today I see the flash of His dividing sword in the homes of the land. Often I am entertained where I feel the strain of it: some of the family are for Christ and some are against Him, and one can almost see the Great Divider standing in the midst. Now, of course, when He said that we were to hate our loved ones He meant it relatively: we are not to love our families less, we are to love Him more. Most of us don't love our families enough. Joseph H. Choate was asked, " If you couldn't be yourself, whom would you rather be? " He answered, " I'd rather be Mrs. Choate's second husband." We need more of that kind of love, to judge by the divorce records these days. And sometimes Christians take a wrong attitude toward unsaved loved ones by trying to act so good that everybody else is embarrassed by the comparison. We are not to try to force spiritual things on sinners. Wives often wonder why husbands resent being talked to about spiritual things. Of course they resent it, for it is pearls before swine. Now, don't tell him that I called him a hog! The point is, don't force deeper spiritual things on unsaved loved ones; pray for them, live the Christ life before them, and make sure that the division in your home is due to your identification with Christ and not to a Pharisaic holier-than-thou attitude on your part.

But Christ does divide homes, and you need not be surprised, for He plainly said He would. A lot of this trouble could be avoided if Christians married in the Lord, but where one gets saved after marriage and the other does not, there is bound to be conflict. You can expect the dividing sword, for He did not come to smooth things over but to call us to Himself, and if we follow Him we need not be surprised if our foes are those of our own household. But let us pray and live for their salvation and make sure that the conflict is because of Christ and not because of ourselves.

Christ divides the professing church. He stands among the candlesticks today and says, " Repent, or else I will come unto thee quickly and fight against them with the sword of my mouth " (Rev. 2: 16). When I stand before church congregations on Sunday morning, I wonder, " How much of all this can stand the test of the Great Divider? " When the choir sings, He knows whether they are making melody in their hearts to the Lord. When the offering is taken, He knows whether they have first given themselves unto the Lord. When the sermon is preached, He knows whether it is in demonstration of the Spirit and of power or whether it is sounding brass and clanging cymbal. When the congregation sings, He knows whether they mean it or whether they are drawing nigh God with their mouths and honoring Him with their lips while their hearts are far from Him. He divides the professing church into professors and possessors, and the test is not church loyalty but our relationship to Him.

There is a great deal of division among Christians and churches today. Some of it is good and some of it is bad. It depends on what causes the division. There was evil division in the Corinthian church, and Paul warns in Romans, " Mark THEM which cause divisions . . . and avoid them " (16: 17). Some divisions are caused by men, their prejudices and bickerings. But Paul says also, " There must be also heresies [sects] among you, that they which

are approved may be made manifest among you " (1 Cor.
11: 19). Three times we read that " there was a division
among the people " on account of Jesus (John 7: 43; 9: 16;
10: 19). There was a division in Iconium on account of
the ministry of Paul and Barnabas (Acts 14: 4). Schisms
caused by men are of the devil, but division caused by
Christ is another matter, and the church has grown by such
division. Every forward movement of the church has been
due to division. The church is the ecclesia, the called-out
ones, and whenever the church becomes cold and worldly
and conventional and settles down in this world, God raises
up a man or movement to call out His faithful people again,
and, of course, that causes division. Suppose Martin Luther
had said, " Oh, well, I don't believe in the church of Rome,
but I'll go along with them and not cause a split." The
Reformation would never have come. If Wesley and Whitefield and Fox and Williams and all of their kind had stayed
in the rut and gone along with the apostate church of their
day in order to avoid offense, Christianity would have died
of dry rot long ago.

There is fast forming today an apostate world church, and
we who believe the Word of God need never expect to be
faithful and avoid division. There may be some question
as to when and how we are to separate, but separate we
eventually must or be put out or else be compromisers.
There are worse things than schism and division. Unity and
harmony and catholicity at the price of principle are a
thousand times worse. It was catholicity that killed Jesus,
a united front that avoided a break with tradition by crucifying the Saviour. There is a united front today that is
crucifying Him afresh. True unity is found through the
fellowship of those who have come out of that united front
to go unto Him without the camp bearing His reproach.
Now, some brethren do not go about this matter in the best
way. Some of them spend more time attacking each other

than fighting the enemy. We must be sure that we divide because of our identification with Christ and not just because we enjoy a fight or want to lead a movement. HE must cause the division, otherwise we belong to " THEM which cause division."

This whole matter of separation should be a question of our identification with Christ, whether it be a matter of church action or individual consecration. There are a lot of so-called " spiritual people " in churches who are not really in love with Christ; they are just in love with their own ideas and their own little clique, and are merely religious snobs. If you do not play cards or dance or go to the movies just in order to glory in your Pharisaic spiritual superiority, that is not Christian separation; but if you do not engage in such things because you are dead and buried and risen with Christ, then it is His sword that divides. Of course, He divides many churches on such issues, but those who have thus separated unto Him must not develop into a clique; they must love and seek to win those who do not so believe and live.

But let us not be frightened with the idea that all division is of the devil. Christ is the Great Divider, and, the darker the times become, the more distinctly will Christ's own followers stand out. If we are faithful to Him we will be distinct enough. We shall not need to bother trying to appear distinct! However, there will be decisions to make as to fellowship with the ungodly, and religious leaders will make us appear selfish and narrow disturbers of the peace. Never mind. That healthy and wholesome schism that grows out of faithfulness to God and His Word has been the life of Christianity through the ages. Better a thousand times the disturbing vitality of the living than the comfortable uniformity of the dead.

Christ divides all mankind, and He divides for all eternity. As I walk the streets, I try to remember that every man or woman is on one side or the other of this Great Divider. If we really believed this, would we not be more zealous to warn men of judgment and call them to the Lord? We talk politics, business, the weather; but how difficult it is to ask them, " On which side of the Great Divider are you? " Don't ask them about the church, for He divides the church. Don't ask them about doctrines, for He divides doctrines. Ask them about Him! A lot of preaching and personal work gets men to looking at each other and at churches but not to Christ. He is the Rock on which men split themselves to the right or left.

And it is an eternal division. He is coming for His saints, who will be caught up to be with Him in the air, and so shall we EVER be with the Lord. At the judgment of the nations He will divide the sheep from the goats. At the judgment of the great white throne those who are not written in the book of life shall be cast into the lake of fire. On that day the only book that will matter will be not the Blue Book nor the bank book nor the church book but the Lamb's Book!

> " Is your name written there?
> On its page white and fair,
> In the book of His Kingdom,
> Is your name written there? "

It is bad to be on the wrong side of anything, but worst of all is to be on the wrong side of Jesus. On which side of the line are you? Come to Him, trust Him, that you may be found in Him, clad in His righteousness alone, faultless to stand before the throne.